STRINDBERG AND MODERNIST THEATRE

Despite the profound influence exerted by August Strindberg on the development of modernist theatre and drama, the myth has persisted that his plays – particularly such later works as *A Dream Play*, *To Damascus*, and *The Ghost Sonata* – are somehow "unperformable." Nothing could be farther from the truth, as this book sets out to demonstrate by providing, for the first time in English, a detailed performance analysis of the major works created after the psychic upheaval Strindberg called his Inferno. Ranging from the early productions of Max Reinhardt and Olof Molander to the reinterpretations of Robert Lepage, Robert Wilson, and Ingmar Bergman in our own day, this study explores the crucial impact that this writer's allusive (and elusive) method of playwriting has had on the changing nature of the theatrical experience. Each chapter ends with a section devoted to innovative Strindberg performances on the contemporary stage.

As a team, the authors have published a wide range of books that include *A History of Scandinavian Theatre* (1996), *Ingmar Bergman: a Life in the Theatre* (1992), *Ibsen's Lively Art* (1989), *Ingmar Bergman: Four Decades in the Theatre* (1982), *Edward Gordon Craig and "The Pretenders"* (1981), and others. Frederick Marker's other books include studies of Hans Andersen, Kjeld Abell, and several editions and translations. Lise-Lone Marker is the author of *David Belasco: Naturalism in the American Theatre* and many articles and chapters on subjects ranging from Elizabethan acting to Swedish cinema.

STRINDBERG AND MODERNIST THEATRE

Post-Inferno Drama on the Stage

FREDERICK J. MARKER
AND
LISE-LONE MARKER

CAMBRIDGE
UNIVERSITY PRESS

PUBLISHED BY THE PRESS SYNDICATE OF THE UNIVERSITY OF CAMBRIDGE
The Pitt Building, Trumpington Street, Cambridge, United Kingdom

CAMBRIDGE UNIVERSITY PRESS
The Edinburgh Building, Cambridge CB2 2RU, UK
40 West 20th Street, New York, NY 10011-4211, USA
477 Williamstown Road, Port Melbourne, VIC 3207, Australia
Ruiz de Alarcón 13, 28014 Madrid, Spain
Dock House, The Waterfront, Cape Town 8001, South Africa

http://www.cambridge.org

First published 2002

Printed in the United Kingdom at the University Press, Cambridge

Typeface Baskerville Monotype 11 / 12.5 pt   *System* LaTeX 2$_\varepsilon$ [TB]

A catalogue record for this book is available from the British Library

ISBN 0 521 62377 4 hardback

CONTENTS

ILLUSTRATIONS

PREFACE

The formative influence of August Strindberg on the development of both modern drama and modern theatre holds the status of a critical truism that no one familiar with the subject would presumably dispute. Yet, paradoxically, one of the sturdiest myths that has attached itself to Strindberg's work, both in his own time and in ours, has been the notion that his plays – particularly the great experimental masterpieces of his post-Inferno period – are somehow "unperformable." Although Strindberg scholarship has flourished in recent years, comparatively little attention has been devoted to the critical analysis of his plays in performance and the consequent relationship between dramaturgy and mise-en-scène. One of the more useful efforts to restore a more balanced understanding of Strindberg's inherent theatricality was made in the monograph on *Miss Julie* and its performance "transcriptions" published some years ago by Egil Törnqvist and Barry Jacobs. Until now, however, no detailed performance study of Strindberg's major post-Inferno works – by which we chiefly mean *A Dream Play*, *To Damascus*, and *The Ghost Sonata* – has been available in English, despite the compelling impact these plays can be said to have had on modernist and postmodernist theatre and theatrical theory. Hence, the present study represents an attempt to fill that gap and, in the process, to dispel the myth of unperformability that has fostered it.

At the heart of the issue is the crucial effect that this writer's allusive (and elusive) method has had on the changing nature of the theatrical experience and the spectator's relationship to it. In spite of the undeniable difficulties they present and the innovative thinking they demand in production, the three plays with which this study is mainly preoccupied have never lost their grip on the imaginations of directors, actors, and designers. Our approach is necessarily selective, however, drawing on representative examples of conceptually significant (or occasionally wrongheaded) interpretations that translate the words on Strindberg's page into the visual and verbal language of the living theatre. In this respect, we feel it is important to give the reader the opportunity to become a kind of spectator, and this is why we have often chosen to furnish more detailed and faceted accounts of a few productions of a particular play, rather than attempting to provide (even if we had been able to compile one) a laundry list of all of its major and recent productions. For reasons that should be obvious, we have not sought to achieve any such inclusive coverage.

Nor has the polemical distinction that is sometimes insisted on between the productions of the so-called establishment theatre and those of the fringe seemed to us to have any relevance to our argument. Susan Einhorn's staging of *A Dream Play* at the Open Space in New York in 1981 was an interesting, provocative conceptualization achieved in a small experimental theatre. But so was Max Reinhardt's 1916 staging of *The Ghost Sonata* at his Kammerspiele in Berlin. And so, too, was Ingmar Bergman's revisitation of the *Sonata* last year in Dramaten's chamber theatre. In the end, the significance of all these productions lies in the light each sheds on the text and the choices each makes in order to bring that text to life for a contemporary audience. While we offer no apology for the prominence inevitably accorded the interpretations of Reinhardt, Bergman, and Olof Molander, the three foremost directors of Strindberg's later plays during the past century, our field of inquiry has nonetheless been wide and ranges from early approaches to the post-Inferno work by Per Lindberg, Evgeny Vakhtangov, and the German expressionists to contemporary reinterpretations by Robert Lepage and Robert Wilson.

The work of other scholars has provided us with an important stimulus. The significance of the line of discussion opened up more than twenty years ago by Richard Bark's Swedish dissertation on the dramaturgical and theatrical implications of Strindberg's "dream-play technique" has not diminished, and the direction we have taken in our own research on Strindberg in performance reflects the positive example set by Bark's pioneering study. Similarly constructive has been the influence exerted by other prominent Scandinavian critics in this area, among them Kela Kvam (in her work on Reinhardt and Strindberg) and Gunnar Ollén (in his concise, commented performance calendars for each of Strindberg's plays). It is to Ollén's work and the supplementary production listings that have been published each year by Strindbergssällskapet (The Strindberg Society) that the reader in search of performance calendars for Strindberg's plays must turn.

Anyone writing about Strindberg in English is virtually bound to feel indebtedness both to the criticism and the translations of Michael Robinson, Evert Sprinchorn, Harry Carlson, and Michael Meyer. We are no exceptions in our admiration for their respective contributions. In particular, the scrupulous Robinson edition of the playwright's letters has made the task of scholars or students working only in English immeasurably more rewarding.

In practical terms, our research in primary sources has been greatly aided by the cooperation of a wide range of institutions and archives, a number of which are named in the list of illustrations or in the notes. Among these, we owe a singular debt of gratitude to the Royal Dramatic Theatre in Stockholm – known to its friends and admirers the world over as Dramaten – where Ann-Christine Jernberg, Dag Kronman, and many others have responded to our requests for sources and yet more sources with unfailing forbearance – and tangible results. On the editorial side, we again have the opportunity to express our warm appreciation to Dr. Victoria L. Cooper of Cambridge University Press for her continued help and encouragement. Not least, we are deeply grateful to the Social Sciences and Humanities Research Council of Canada for research grants awarded in support of this study.

Before Inferno: Strindberg and nineteenth-century theatre

It could be said of August Strindberg, as it has often been said of Yeats, that he wrote himself out of the nineteenth century and into the twentieth. The great period of experimentation that produced the dream plays and the chamber plays began just before the turn of the century, in the aftermath of the massive psychic upheaval Strindberg described as his Inferno (1894–97). Of the plays written before that personal crisis, only a small handful – notably *Miss Julie*, *The Father*, and *Master Olof* – have sustained a subsequent history of major productions. All three of these, moreover, point forward and are linked in one way or another to the plays and poetics of his post-Inferno period. All this having been said, however, it would nevertheless be misleading to overlook altogether Strindberg's apprenticeship in the nineteenth-century theatre and its conventions. The earlier plays and their first productions laid an important groundwork of experience. It was from this basis that his dramaturgy and theatre poetics developed, at a time when the new influence of modern drama and theatre was becoming an increasingly dominant force.

"It is impossible to set up rules for theatrical art, but it ought to be contemporary." This statement, reiterated many times by Strindberg in varying contexts during the course of his career, points to a fundamental characteristic of his theatre practice. Almost from the outset, his art became a restless search for new forms capable of meeting the changing demands of the consciousness of the time, as seen from his uniquely personal point of view. Both as a playwright and as a theorist, Strindberg kept in touch with the newest directions and developments in theatre and drama, ready both to absorb and reshape them in his own way. As the arch rebel and social iconoclast, he was the ardent champion of a comprehensive revitalization of the theatre which, by the end of the nineties, he was convinced could only be accomplished through a redefinition of the nature of the theatrical experience itself. During the decades preceding that realization, his idea of theatre underwent radical change. This process was not, however, one of continuous, linear, or even consistent development. Instead, its course was defined by an oscillating succession of experiments that led, gradually but surely, to a total rejection of the accepted conventions of stage illusion and dramatic construction, as inadequate means of expressing the mystical and visionary aspects of life that, to an increasing extent, he came to regard as the true fabric of reality.

During a brief, unhappy period as an aspiring actor in 1869, Strindberg had his first taste of the theatrical climate and repertory of the day. His "debut" at Dramaten came in a revival of Bjørnstjerne Bjørnson's *Maria Stuart in Scotland*, in which he played a messenger with fewer than a dozen lines to speak. A grander scheme, to make his real stage debut as the stormy romantic hero Karl Moor in Schiller's *The Robbers*, predictably came to nought. He quickly found his footing as a playwright, however, and his first produced play appeared in 1870. This was a one-act verse drama called *In Rome* [*I Rom*], a Scribean vignette of anecdotal history depicting an incident in the life of the renowned sculptor Bertel Thorvaldsen, who as a young artist is saved from despair when an unexpected benefactor (Thomas Hope) commissions the famous Jason statue. Acted at Dramaten by an exceptional cast that included Axel Elmlund as an elegant, elegiac Thorvaldsen, this anonymous "Swedish original" enjoyed an auspicious run of eleven performances in the 1870–71 season. At the start of his career as a playwright, Strindberg was strongly influenced by the traditional romantic preoccupation with history, saga, and folklore that had also characterized the early work of both Ibsen and Bjørnson a generation earlier. The influence of his great Scandinavian predecessors is plainly evident in *The Outlaw* [*Den fredlöse*], a new one-acter Strindberg brought to the stage at Dramaten the next season. The theme of this saga drama is the conflict of Christianity and heathenism in twelfth-century Iceland. This time, however, the play met a chilly reception. Alfred Hanson, a decorative but rather wooden actor with a soporific delivery, was no match for the towering Viking hero Thorfinn ("a titan, a Prometheus who struggles against the gods"), and the 22-year-old dramatist learned a useful lesson about a play's dependence upon the exigencies of performance.

More than nine years elapsed before another Strindberg play reached the Stockholm stage. Although he submitted the first prose version of *Master Olof* [*Mäster Olof*] to Dramaten as early as 1872, the theatre's readers were reluctant to recommend a work in which the historical characters seemed so altered from their traditional conceptions – though this was obviously the author's whole point in this early masterpiece. At Nya teatern, where a bolder artistic policy came to prevail, the pioneering manager–director Ludvig Josephson eventually accepted the original prose version of the play, preferring it above the verse version published in 1878. The prominent naturalistic director August Lindberg staged the premiere of this sprawling historical chronicle at Josephson's theatre at the end of 1881. Strindberg's typically revisionist view of familiar figures of sixteenth-century Swedish history depicts Olaus Petri, biblical translator and influential champion of Luther's teachings, as an unheroic protagonist, a vacillating, hyperreflective religious revolutionary who, unlike the fiery and uncompromising rebel Gert Bookprinter, betrays himself and his beliefs. In terms of its style, the play's loose form, multiple changes of scene, and incisive use of realistic detail also challenged accepted conventions. The centre of energy in Lindberg's riveting six-hour production was the larger-than-life characterization of Gert created by the young Emil Hillberg, whose demonic fanaticism and black humour provided a striking contrast to the weak-willed Olof of William Engelbrecht. The play made Hillberg the new star of Swedish theatre, while its author at last found himself acclaimed as one of the foremost dramatists of the early 1880s.

Strindberg's interest in the history-play genre would reassert itself in his post-Inferno work, but in the early years he also experimented with the use of period setting in a different way, as a framing device for domestic dramas of married life that reflected his own initially contented but increasingly harrowing emotional life with his first wife, the strong-willed actress Siri von Essen. She played the staunchly loyal Margaretha in *The Secret of the Guild* [*Gillets hemlighet*] at Dramaten in 1880, in a production that marked a crucial step toward her husband's definitive breakthrough as a playwright the following year. Reminiscent of Ibsen's *The Pretenders*, this four-act play dramatizes the rival claims of two fifteenth-century master builders vying for the honour of completing the cathedral at Uppsala. One of them is a man who possesses the true strength of a great calling; the other, his own son, is the dishonest and inept pretender who is ultimately thwarted in his ambition when the tower he has constructed collapses. A closing scene in which Margaretha, wife of the humbled upstart, forgives and (in his own words) "redeems" her repentant husband provided a consoling outcome. The Strindbergian theme of marriage as an emotional battleground is more strongly stated in *Sir Bengt's Wife* [*Herr Bengts hustru*], a five-act medieval pastiche in which Siri von Essen again enjoyed great success as Margit in its production at Nya teatern in 1883. She is Strindberg's alternative to Nora in a play that quite evidently presents an answer of sorts to *A Doll's House*. After the rebellious Margit has deserted husband and child and has attempted suicide, the marital combatants are at last reconciled in the end, as a love stronger than either rational logic or individual will prevails over the inevitable warfare of the sexes.

Lucky Per's Journey [*Lycko-Pers resa*], which proved to be one of Strindberg's most popular successes when produced at Nya teatern at the end of 1883, also employs a vaguely medieval setting, but this fairy-tale fantasy denotes a move in an entirely new and significant direction. In this work the playwright embarked, as it were, on a drama of pilgrimage that he continued years later in the much harsher, more phantasmagorical atmosphere of *The Keys to Heaven* [*Himmelrikets nycklar*, 1892], a fantasia in which a heartbroken smith searching for his dead children joins an aging and forgetful Saint Peter in a hopeless quest for the keys to heaven. The culmination of Strindberg's artistic pilgrimage would be the great journey plays of the post-Inferno period. Unlike these other works, however, *Lucky Per's Journey* retains a bitter-sweet fairy-tale quality that is resonant with echoes of the major works of Scandinavian romanticism – Adam Oehlenschläger's *Aladdin*, Ibsen's *Peer Gynt*, and not least the stories and fairy-tale plays of Hans Christian Andersen. After young Per leaves the belfry in which he has been raised, he wanders the world in search of happiness, discovering in the process that nothing is what he had imagined it to be. Instead, like many an Andersen figure with a wishing ring and a fairy godmother, he learns that the realization of his dreams of gold and honour and power brings with it only bitter disillusionment.

The fleeting, dreamlike transitions in this play, its replacement of the logic of reality with the imaginative logic of a fairy tale, and its invocation of a realism of the unreal are all signposts that point ahead to the dramaturgy of the mature dream plays. As it was originally conceived and performed, however, *Lucky Per* belongs squarely in spirit to the romantic theatre of pictorial illusion. In its use of transparencies, startling transformations, and a multiplicity of elaborately representational settings for its short, kaleidoscopic scenes, it took full advantage of the spectacular stage effects and mechanical wizardry of which the painted wing-and-border stage of the nineteenth century was capable. Consider, for example, the second-act *changement à vue* in which "a snow-covered forest" at dawn, with "an ice-covered brook" running across the stage in the foreground, is transformed "from winter to summer: the ice melts on the brook and it runs freely over the stones, while the sun shines over the entire scene."

Eventually, Strindberg would come to look upon a realistic representation of such an effect on the stage as "wasted effort," simply because the careful, detailed setting required to bring it off convincingly only detracted from the dreamlike mood it endeavoured to convey. Before his crucial reorientation toward simplification, however, he had to pass through a phase coloured, as he later writes, by a "naturalistic taste, adapted to the materialistic objectives of the age, [that] strove for realistic accuracy."[1] During this earlier stage in his development, his primary concern thus became the intensification of an illusion of objective, credible reality in the theatre.

Always closely attuned to new theatrical directions – and always ready to acknowledge debts of literary or theatrical influence – Strindberg was preoccupied from the early 1880s with the emergence of naturalism and its quest for a "new formula" for art. With *The Father* [*Fadren*, 1887] his writing underwent a radical change that he was certain represented the formula for which "the young Frenchmen" were still searching. For this playwright, the term "naturalism" was synonymous from the outset with what he comes to describe, in "On Modern Theatre and Modern Drama" (1889), as "the great style, the deep probing of the human soul." He was never convinced by the merely photographic aspects of the movement or by its sometimes exaggerated insistence on the reproduction of the details of surface reality. "If a woman is seduced in a hothouse," he writes dryly, "it isn't necessary to relate the seduction to all the potted plants you can find there and list them all by name."[2] Instead, what he calls greater naturalism is that "which seeks out the points where the great battles are fought, which loves to see what you do not see every day, which delights in the struggle between natural forces, whether these forces are called love and hate, rebellious or social instinct, which finds the beautiful or ugly unimportant if only it is great."[3] In this interpretation, the elements of external verisimilitude in the naturalistic style serve only as a means of achieving an intensification of dramatic mood and conflict.

In this way, the unrelenting struggle for dominance and survival that rages between Laura and the Captain, the titanic contestants in *The Father*, acquired added horror for its first audiences by being so concretely anchored in a contemporary bourgeois milieu they found familiar. Yet the conflict in the play quickly takes on an added dimension, bursting the bounds of mere realism and confronting us with a harrowing dramatic image of hell as mutual psychic torment. The suggestion that the Captain is not the real father of his only child festers and grows to an obsession that severs his ties with objective reality, undermines the basis of his very existence, and ends by bringing on the fatal stroke he suffers when his female persecutors lure him onto a straitjacket. But here, as in the subsequent plays of gender warfare, the primary emphasis is not on the customary naturalistic interaction of character and a convincingly lifelike environment. In *The Father*, as in such one-acters as *Creditors* [*Fordringsägare*, 1888] and *The Bond* [*Bandet*, 1892] as well as in both parts of *The Dance of Death* [*Dödsdansen*, 1900], the sex wars take place in a context of detailed verisimilitude. However, their full theatrical impact derives from the evocation of a wrenching, nightmarish atmosphere that transcends this reality, yet nevertheless remains familiar by virtue of a tightly controlled realistic technique. What one might call an almost Ibsenian blend of naturalism and symbolism ("super-naturalism," O'Neill later chose to call it) becomes even more evident in *The Dance of Death*, an anomalous work that, although written after the Inferno, still retains the style and features of the earlier marriage plays to which it is generically linked.

Zola, the principal spokesman for naturalism in the theatre of the late nineteenth century, appears not to have been wholly convinced by Strindberg's idea of a "greater" naturalism. In a letter (December 14, 1887) occasioned by the publication of the French translation of *The Father*, he objected that "the Captain without a name [and] the others who are almost entirely abstract figures do not give me as powerful a sense of reality as I demand."[4] The inaccuracy of Zola's statement about the namelessness of the Captain (whose name is Adolf) has often been noticed. Equally misleading is his broader judgment that the play lacks a strong "sense of reality." It was precisely the shock of its realistic immediacy that almost completely overshadowed the reception of its first performance, which opened at Casino Theatre in Copenhagen in November 1887 amidst a storm of controversy. Directed by Hans Riber Hunderup, the production became, above all, an ideological battleground of opposing tastes. To demonstrate his solidarity, Georg Brandes even took the unusual step of attending rehearsals. "From the very outset one could see how numerous the Strindbergians, or those whose natures were more or less in sympathy with the Strindbergian tendency, were in attendance: the applause which was heard from beginning to end was truly enthusiastic," the critic for *Nationaltidende* (November 14, 1887) observed. "Whether this success will last more than a very few evenings remains quite another matter. So far as we are concerned, we think not." Despite their praise of the play's technique, most of its first reviewers took strong exception to the unrelenting despair of Strindberg's vision. *Berlingske Tidende* summed up the reaction of a large conservative majority impervious to a fervent campaign by the Brandes brothers on behalf of Strindberg and modernism: "Despite the talent revealed in the technical construction of the play, it nevertheless remains a bitter, unpoetic fruit on the arid tree of realism."

At the eye of the critical hurricane was the unnerving straitjacket scene. "How far have we actually drifted, when that grim instrument of the insane asylum, the straitjacket, has managed to become a means of gaining effect on the stage?" demanded the angry critic for *Dagbladet* (November 16). "An uglier, more revolting scene has probably never been presented in a Danish theatre. Those who only read the play have no conception of how incredibly nerve-racking this sight is. . . . The mood of the real audience – those who had not attended a demonstration – was oppressed and indignant." This particular observer's logic is interesting: precisely because a play like *The Father* speaks to everyone in a theatre, modern drama "has no right to use such unrefined and brutal means to achieve effect," he insists. Although *Aftonbladet* (November 16) might argue that "in its scenic effectiveness it ranks on a level with the very best in modern dramatic literature," the harrowing straitjacket scene remained the focus of conservative umbrage. "The drama is bleak enough as it is, so crushing and depressing that this scene is the drop that makes the cup run over," the reviewer for *Nationaltidende* declared, while his like-minded colleague at *Dags-Telegrafen* added: "We can well understand why individual spectators stood up this evening during the third act and left the auditorium."

Although Hunderup's actors, accustomed to the light Casino repertory, lacked the requisite strength and technique for this demanding task, their performances, with Hunderup and his future wife Johanne Krum in the leading roles, won high praise. "When one must daily hold an audience through the aid of exaggerated outward action with many gestures and grimaces, it is no small problem when, for once, one must return to the evenness and naturalness that are the devices of all good plays," Edvard Brandes observed in *Politiken*. He was especially impressed, however, by the able portrayal of Laura, "acted with a natural and heavy tone of voice that has an extremely intense effect." Strindberg's own conception of the proper performance style for his play was, at this time, characterized by a similar emphasis on a subdued naturalistic approach. "Act the play as Lindberg acted Ibsen; that is, not tragedy, not comedy, but something in between," he wrote in a letter (December 23, 1887) addressed to the management of Nya teatern, which was preparing to stage the Swedish premiere. "Don't take too fast a tempo as we did to begin with here at the Casino. Rather, let it creep forward quietly, evenly, until it gathers momentum of its own accord towards the last act. Exception: the Captain's speeches when his *idée fixe* has broken out. They should be spoken rapidly, abruptly, spat out, repeatedly breaking the atmosphere."[5] The role must be played with "the superior, self-mocking, slightly cynical air of a man of the world," Strindberg wrote to the young novelist Axel Lundegård a month before the Hunderup premiere (October 17, 1887): "This is what is modern in my tragedy, and woe betide me and the clown if he goes overboard and acts *The Robbers* in 1887. No shrieks, no sermons. Subtly, calmly, with resignation – as an otherwise healthy spirit accepts his modern fate in the form of erotic passion."

Two decades later, Strindberg's ideas about both acting and the nature of the theatrical experience in general had changed drastically. By the time *The Father* was revived at his own Intimate Theatre in Stockholm in 1908, he was essentially finished with naturalism. Instead, he urged August Falck, who directed the production and also acted the Captain, to stage the play in an abstract, simplified setting of dark drapes so that, in his words, it would "be lifted out of its everyday atmosphere and become tragedy in the grand style; the characters will be sublimated, ennobled, and appear as from another world." He also intended the acting to develop this idea further: "*The Father* should be played as tragedy. Grand, broad gestures, loud voices . . . let loose the passions."[6] Falck was having none of this, however, and both photos of the Intima production and the 1911 film based on it confirm a style of staging and performance firmly anchored in the naturalistic tradition. When the play finally reached the stage at Dramaten in 1915, the "appealingly quiet sadness" of Emil Hillberg's meditative interpretation of the Captain likewise harked back to the playwright's earlier vision of a rigorously subdued, unhistrionic tone and atmosphere.

"Perhaps you know that I have no sympathy with the abstract," Zola had written in the letter to Strindberg about *The Father*. "I demand to know everything about the characters' positions in life so that one can touch and perceive them, sense them in their own atmosphere." Possibly as a consequence of this letter, adherence to the Zolaist principles of dramatic character became more pronounced in *Miss Julie* (*Fröken Julie*) than in any other Strindberg play. He himself considered this work "the first naturalistic tragedy in Swedish drama" – "'*Ceci datera!*' = this play will go down in the annals," he added, with characteristic directness, in his submission letter of August 10, 1888 to the publisher Karl Otto Bonnier. In the long Preface, added for distribution to the patrons of the Théâtre Libre in Paris in 1893, he seems consciously to have set out to promulgate the ideas of theatrical reform advocated by Zola and Antoine, director of the French production. In so doing, he formulated what has since come to be regarded as perhaps the clearest summary of the aims and methods of the naturalistic style of theatre. In performance, Strindberg wanted the spectator to experience the drama of the Midsummer Eve seduction and suicide of the aristocratic protagonist as an unbroken slice of living reality. In order for an audience to respond in this way, the developing confrontation between Julie and her father's valet Jean must remain undisturbed by an intermission that would disrupt "the suggestive influence of the dramatist–hypnotist." To intensify the illusion of reality further, the large kitchen in which the action takes place must be fully three-dimensional, thereby eliminating "the effort of believing in painted saucepans." Yet at the same time, Strindberg describes a setting that should be impressionistically conceived, with a use of asymmetry that stimulates our imagination so that "we complete the picture ourselves." By advocating the elimination of footlights and heavy make-up and by introducing strong side-lighting to accentuate eye and facial (i.e., psychological) expressiveness, he sought to create a close-up drama of subtler reactions "mirrored more in the face than in gestures and sound." Following Antoine's lead and often using his vocabulary, he called for the actor to disregard the audience seated beyond the invisible fourth wall and to perform within, rather than in front of, the setting/environment. In this way each scene would be played in "that part of the stage the action dictates." I do not "dream of seeing the full back of an actor throughout an important scene," he writes, "but I do fervently wish that vital scenes should not be performed next to the prompter's box, as duets designed to elicit applause."[7]

Although its views on theatrical production are largely restatements of existing naturalistic theory, the dramaturgical arguments advanced in the Preface to *Miss Julie* often combine aspects of the naturalistic aesthetic with observations that point in a new, distinctly postnaturalistic direction. A complexity of motives – psychological, biological, environmental, hereditary – customarily underlies the behaviour of a naturalistically conceived character; yet the "split and vacillating" characters envisioned by Strindberg – "conglomerations of past and present stages of culture, bits out of books and newspapers, scraps of humanity, torn shreds of once fine clothing now turned to rags" – are potentially Pirandellian in their characterlessness. His advocacy of a meandering, non-sequential pattern of dialogue, mirroring the randomness and casualness of everyday conversation, anticipates the dialogue of free association in Chekhov's work. Not least, the allusions in the Preface to musical composition and thematics become fully meaningful in Strindberg's own dream plays and chamber plays.

Strindberg conceived *Miss Julie* to be performed by a small experimental theatre. The founding of Antoine's Théâtre Libre in 1887 had sparked widespread interest in the concept of a free, independent theatre as a venue for trying out new plays and production methods. Strindberg, who had entertained the notion of a theatre of his own as far back as 1876, was immediately attracted by Antoine's model and approached the energetic Ibsen champion August Lindberg with a proposal that they collaborate to form an independent touring company. His sales pitch was as dynamic as always: "You can't go on for long with Ibsen; for he probably won't write much more, and his particular genre is on the way out . . . He can do his thing, and we ours!" Strindberg's proposal, contained in his long letter of June 3, 1887, was to start a small touring theatre devoted to a repertory made up exclusively of his own works: "We'd never be short of plays, for I can write a one-acter in two days," he reassured Lindberg, to whom all the leading male parts were to be tailored. Siri von Essen was to have all the female leads – but, he adds, "if you want your wife along, I'll write one role for her and one for my wife, alternately, but always with one for you!" His suggestions were meant to be as practical as possible: "I shall write the plays so that it won't be necessary to lug along any costumes, sets, or props." A revolution of the kind envisioned by Antoine and his followers was not the ostensible objective of Strindberg's undertaking: "I have no dreams of transforming or reforming the theatre, for that's impossible. It can only be modernized a little!"

Nearly two years later, when Strindberg finally did succeed in establishing his own Scandinavian Experimental Theatre in Denmark (where he resided from late 1887 to 1889), his venture survived only a week. The small troupe of amateurs and professionals (notably Siri von Essen and Hans Riber Hunderup) set up quarters in Dagmar Theatre, one of Copenhagen's leading private theatres. However, only a day before the scheduled premiere of *Miss Julie*, the event that was to have launched the enterprise, the public censor banned the play on account of its "daring" subject matter. Undaunted, Strindberg's experimental theatre quickly changed plans, opening on the Dagmar stage one week later (March 9,

1889) with a triple bill that included *Creditors* and two short pieces written for the occasion, *The Stronger* (*Den starkare*) and *Pariah* (*Paria*). For practical as well as artistic reasons, Strindberg created all three of these works as performance texts for a small company with a minimum of technical and financial resources. *Creditors* he described as "a naturalistic tragedy, better than *Miss Julie*, with three characters, a table and two chairs, and no sunrise." This popular but perilously contrived three-hander was, however, no success when first attempted. Hunderup was a suitably cynical and worldly Gustav, the vengeful ex-husband who exposes his former wife's inner ruthlessness and perfidy. But Adolf, the adoring spouse who is felled by a stroke when he overhears their vicious confrontation, was too much for the popular Danish writer Gustav Wied, who made his shaky debut as an amateur actor in the role. "People laughed till they had tears in their eyes as the small, slightly built author wriggled about like a worm in a monstrosity of an armchair," a reviewer for *Vort Land* declared.[8] But not all was lost for Strindberg's little ensemble. His wife was very effective as the talky Mrs. X in *The Stronger*, while Hunderup's rendering of X, the inadvertent murderer who outwits his would-be blackmailer in *Pariah*, was a masterpiece that took its place in the regular Dagmar repertory.

As for *Miss Julie* itself, the ban on public performances compelled its world premiere (March 14, 1889) to take place as a private showing for 150 spectators, presented on a makeshift stage in the student union at the University of Copenhagen. Siri Strindberg played a subdued Julie opposite the polite Jean of Viggo Schiwe. "She is too cold, much too cold, and one gets no impression at all of the kind of woman who would seduce a man like Jean," complained a correspondent for the Stockholm daily *Dagens Nyheter* (March 18, 1889). This observer also found that Schiwe "hardly suggested a servant; his manner was much more that of a gentleman or a *viveur*."[9] Despite the primitive production conditions, however, Strindberg's demands for a credibly three-dimensional stage environment appear to have been met. The setting "looked surprisingly like a real kitchen," admitted the critic for *Dagens Nyheter*. "A plate rack, a kitchen table, a speaking tube to the floor above, a big stove with rows of copper pots above it – in short, everything is there, presenting the living image of an actual kitchen." While much else in this play's interpretation would change during the course of its long performance history, its solidly representational setting – icon of the naturalistic belief in environment as a silent character in the drama – has usually remained an indispensable feature of any revival. Not least in the 1951 film of *Miss Julie* made by Alf Sjöberg, one of the foremost directors of this play in the theatre, Kristin's kitchen stands as a vivid reminder of the power of a naturalistically conceived environment as a symbolic force that is at the same time a reality as tangible and practical as the stove on which she fries Jean's supper.

Although *Miss Julie* is probably still the play most commonly associated with Strindberg's name, the naturalistic revolution it helped to ferment soon ceased to hold the playwright's interest. Even by the time his work had reached Paris and the Théâtre Libre in 1893, Strindberg himself had stopped writing plays altogether. Indeed, as Inga-Stina Ewbank observes in an essay on his avid receptiveness to the influence of Shakespeare, his career at that point "looked like that of a naturalist who, after *The Father*, *Miss Julie* and *Creditors*, had written himself into a minimalist corner with plays like *The Stronger* and then fallen silent. . . ." Yet, as Ewbank goes on to point out, "possibly the outstanding Strindbergian characteristic is a continuous growing and renewing, so that it is quite useless to speak of his 'formative' years, since he was forever forming and re-forming his art."[10] And so when he resumed his theatre work at the end of the century, following the darkest time in his life, it was with a very different style of performance and an entirely new kind of revolution in mind.

Toward a new theatre: *To Damascus*

Although the significance of the biographical element has been greatly overstated in traditional Strindberg criticism, it is nevertheless a fact that the wrenching mental crisis through which the playwright passed during the mid-1890s – which he called his Inferno – precipitated a sweeping renewal in his art and particularly in his attitude toward the whole question of theatrical illusion on the stage. In a letter to three of his children, dated May 24, 1898, he describes Part I of *To Damascus* [*Till Damaskus*], the first play he wrote after this shattering psychological ordeal, as a conscious and radical departure from what he had done before – "a new genre, fantastic and brilliant like *Lucky Per*, but with a contemporary setting and with a completely real background." The full reality to which he refers, however, has nothing in common with the external verisimilitude that had been the hallmark of his naturalistic dramas a decade earlier. In none of Strindberg's post-Inferno plays is there, in fact, any hard and fast distinction drawn between what is "real" and what is not. Herein lies the essence of the difficulty facing any director who attempts to stage these plays. Life, for the father of dramatic expressionism, *is* a dream, and so the dream (the play) is life itself. Works such as *A Dream Play* or *To Damascus* are not intellectual comments on "the dreamlike nature of reality"; they are projected images of a psychic dynamism, an exteriorization of *what it feels like* to experience life in this particular way. Hence, perhaps the greatest challenge facing any interpreter of Strindberg's later work on the stage is to articulate the fundamental doubleness of its poetic vision. The problem is to project a perception of the dreamlike quality of reality that is always conjoined with the sharply insistent reality of the dream.

To Damascus, which charts the spiritual journey of its nameless protagonist through a kaleidoscopic succession of "stations" on the road toward an ambiguous salvation, is thus Strindberg's first dream play. Like *A Dream Play* itself, its governing motif is that of repetition and recurrence. At the end of Part I, the pilgrimage of the Unknown [*Den Okände*] "begins again at the same point as the action stops, and where it began," Strindberg wrote to Gustaf af Geijerstam, the first person to read the new drama, on March 17, 1898. The protagonist's outward journey scrolls through eight scenes that lead him to the Asylum, the pivotal episode that Strindberg's letter likens to "the spine of a book that shuts upon itself and encloses the action." The last eight scenes then take the Unknown back along the same road in reverse order, as the action "rebounds back through the pilgrimage, the relearning, the eating of one's words."

When *To Damascus I* appeared in print in 1898, its episodic form and multiple localities convinced most critics that it was an unperformable closet drama. Strindberg himself was undaunted ("the play must be performed: *c'est du theatre!*"), and in Emil Grandinson he was fortunate to find a director with an exceptional sensitivity to the complex inner life of the new work. "Grandinson went beyond [the naturalistic director Harald] Molander's 'externals' and admitted I was right when I was right, seeing that the effect or the impact of the play depended on something other than what was piquant in the situation and the scenic effects," Strindberg later wrote in his *Open Letters to the Intimate Theatre* (*LIT*, 127). Like the playwright himself, Grandinson was well versed in the newest developments and currents in modernist theatre, represented in the writings of Georg Fuchs (*Die Schaubühne der Zukunft*), Adolphe Appia (*La Mise en scène du drame Wagnerien*), and Gordon Craig (*On the Art of the Theatre*). The principles of suggestion, stylization, and simplification eventually advocated by these reformers were already discernible formative impulses in Grandinson's *Damascus* mise-en-scène ("something new and a masterpiece by way of direction," thought the author). These ideas also continued to influence him subsequently in productions of such diverse Strindberg plays as *Easter* [*Påsk*] in 1901, *Karl XII* the following year, *The Last Knight* [*Siste riddaren*] in 1909, and a revival of *The Black Glove* [*Svarta handsken*] in 1911.

To Damascus was written at a time when concepts of theatrical illusion and stage setting were acquiring new meaning, radically at odds with the naturalistic ethos promulgated by Strindberg himself only a few years earlier in his Preface to *Miss Julie*. Appia sums up the view of the New Stagecraft in a single sentence: "Scenic illusion is the living presence of the actor." In one of his most famous examples, in which he discusses the staging of Wagner's *Siegfried*, he takes aim at the absurd attempt by a designer or director to create a "real" forest on the stage. "We no longer seek," he writes, "to give the illusion of a *forest* but that of a *man* in the atmosphere of a forest. Reality here is a man, alongside which no other illusion matters."[1] An interview with Strindberg, published in *Svenska Dagbladet* (January 21, 1899) to mark his fiftieth birthday, makes it clear that the playwright was fully attuned to the modernist views of the New Stagecraft. "I don't want to use ordinary theatre decorations for my new plays," he told the Stockholm paper. "All these old-fashioned theatrical rags must go! I only want a painted background representing a room, a forest, or whatever it may be, or perhaps a background could be produced by a shadow picture painted on glass and projected onto a white sheet."

Strindberg's underlying concept for his *Damascus* cycle was, in fact, rooted from the beginning in his idea of using projection effects to simplify the staging and facilitate the rapid, dreamlike succession of scenes through which the Unknown passes on his journey. Another of the letters to Geijerstam (October 17, 1898) actually suggests that scene changes could be accomplished entirely "by lighting if the scenery is kept in an abstract, shadow-like, colourless tone, which is in keeping with the play." Fully ten years earlier, Strindberg's imagination had been fired by the prospect of replacing conventional painted backdrops with projected pictures. In 1889, while an adaptation of his novel *The People of Hemsö* [*Hemsöborna*] was being staged at a small popular theatre in Stockholm, he had occasion to write to the director August Lindberg about plans for a new play, "half fairy tale, dealing with the French Revolution and using mainly a large magic lantern" as an evocative and economical means of recreating the episodes of history on the stage.[2] Later, like so many of the other symbolist artists of his day, he became captivated by the fleeting, dreamlike effects produced in the shadow plays he saw in Paris at Henri Rivière's famous cabaret theatre, Le Chat Noir. This influence seems to have aroused his renewed interest in experimenting with projected scenery in his post-Inferno plays, in a conscious effort to achieve a simpler, "dematerialized" atmosphere on the stage.

Another aspect of Strindberg's plan to adopt a new, distinctly non-naturalistic style of performance for *To Damascus* derived from his keen interest in the so-called Shakespeare Bühne. In conjunction with a reduction of scenery, costumes, and props to their bare and meaningful essentials, he also advocated the adoption of a neutral platform stage ("something in the style of Shakespeare's time") to counteract the heavily photographic reproduction of parlours and kitchens that filled the stages of his day. "All this theatre nonsense that now overburdens the stage and weighs down the play without increasing believability must be eliminated," he declared in his birthday interview in *Svenska Dagbladet*.

"It is the play itself, the dialogue, the plot that must capture the audience and create the illusion." The latter statement sounds suspiciously like the venerable old saw about the "spoken scenery" created by dialogue alone on Shakespeare's otherwise "bare" stage. In this respect, Strindberg joined theatre reformers from Yeats and William Poel to Jacques Copeau in the shared assumption that a return to the lost "purity" of the Elizabethan stage (as they imagined it to have been) was the only effective antidote to the ills of naturalistic theatre. In particular, the Shakespeare Stage that had been created in Munich in 1889 by Karl von Perfall, Karl Lautenschläger, and Jocza Savits provided Strindberg with a favourite illustration of his own aims and views. An annotated copy of Savits' book, *Die Shakespeare-Bühne in München* (1899) had a place in his personal library. This nineteenth-century version of an Elizabethan stage impressed him deeply as a theatrical model, to which he was to return many times in his continuous campaign for a new, simplified approach to stage illusion. As we shall see, however, substantive and revealing practical differences existed between the von Perfall experiment and the modification of it eventually adopted by Grandinson and Strindberg for the first production of *To Damascus I.*

In general, the Shakespeare Stage erected in Munich was a far more complex hybrid than Strindberg's idealized vision of a simple, naked platform might suggest. One of the earliest and most detailed accounts of the project was compiled by the Danish director William Bloch, who had been dispatched to Bavaria in the summer of 1891 to study the new stage form and report his findings to the management of the Royal Theatre in Copenhagen.[3] Von Perfall's reconstructed proscenium stage at the Hoftheater was designed mainly to handle the rapid alternation of scenes in Shakespearean drama. The fairly elaborate structure comprised three distinct acting areas. A forestage or apron, from which five steps descended to the floor of the auditorium, was built out over the orchestra pit. Behind the proscenium arch, an unlocalized "middle stage" was enclosed at the sides by stylized canvas hangings. The rear wall of this stage consisted of a permanent curtained arch, creating a kind of second proscenium with openings at the top and sides to be used as windows, doors, or an upper gallery. Behind this arch lay an inner stage, described in Bloch's report as "a miniature theatre of its own, with its own settings, its own front curtain, and its own stage floor," raised three steps above the level of the main stage. A painted backcloth was used to depict the location of each scene, and a pair of side wings could supplement this cloth to increase the illusion of place. When viewed in conjunction with the middle stage, the setting in the background thus served to anchor the action in a particular location, be it a garden, a room, a street, or wherever.

Bloch, who was acclaimed for his meticulously detailed naturalistic productions of Ibsen, Shakespeare, and Holberg, was understandably disconcerted by the comparative bareness of von Perfall's stage. Because only the inner stage offered "any real sense of localization," he argued, the curtained opening to it was closed only "on those comparatively rare occasions when the spectators are in no doubt about where a given scene is taking place." The only real advantage of the experiment, in his opinion, was the ease with which it overcame the technical difficulties associated with multiple changes of scene, thereby making it preferable for plays written "before the advent of modern staging principles" or else for works "not conceived by their author for performance." For modern plays, "which for the most part avail themselves of the full resources of contemporary stagecraft," Bloch could find no real use for von Perfall's method. "There can be no doubt," he reported to the Royal Theatre management, "that it is distinctly inferior to the modern theatre when it comes to scenic illusion; it gives the actors none of the support they enjoy to such a great extent in a modern mise-en-scène."

It was precisely this naturalistic line of reasoning which, by experimenting freely with new methods of staging, both Strindberg and Grandinson hoped to displace in the first production of *To Damascus I* at Dramaten (November 19, 1900). The stage itself was divided horizontally to create the impression of two stages, an inner and an outer, joined by three connecting steps. The raised inner stage was framed by a more austere version of the second proscenium arch used by von Perfall in his Shakespeare Stage. Tor Hedberg, one of the most influential of the Stockholm critics, likened the picturesque effect to "the crumbling wall of an ancient theatre, pierced by a wide, vaulted opening. Above the wall one saw a piece of sky, where in the night scenes a starry pattern was visible" (*Svenska Dagbladet*, November 20, 1900). Rather than emulating the alternation of playing areas and the in-depth figure compositions favoured by von Perfall in Munich, however, Grandinson's mise-en-scène placed the entire action on the raised stage-upon-the-stage, defined by its vaulted, curtainless arch. In doing so it succeeded in projecting an impression of unreality, distance, and dream. "The figures who appear here become diminutive," observed the critic for *Aftonbladet* (November 20), "and in the half light, which eliminates contours and often leaves the faces in shadow, it is easy to imagine oneself in an hallucinatory state induced by

fever." In this way, as Richard Bark has argued, the spectators themselves
became transformed into "dreamers" of the dream[4] – though it must be
added that it is the Unknown who remains the controlling consciousness
through which the events of the play are perceived.

The period in which Strindberg was writing his post-Inferno plays
was – as the plays themselves reflect – also a time of rapid changes and
advances in stage technology. The whole area of stage lighting is a particular case in point. The creative power of sculptural and expressive
lighting, to which both Appia and Craig attach such importance in their
theories, ultimately depended upon the technical innovations necessary
to make such lighting a practical reality. Although electric lighting had
been introduced at Dramaten only two years before the premiere of *To
Damascus*, Grandinson made effective use of the new medium in establishing atmosphere and creating lighting effects.[5] Red, blue, yellow, and
white lamps attached to five battens above the stage replaced the usual
side lighting. Although only the nightmarish Asylum scene contained
lighting effects that were overtly expressionistic, most of the other lighting changes and nuances throughout the production combined symbolic
weighting with a realistic indication of weather, time of day, or the like
(usually not found in the stage directions but extrapolated by Grandinson
from Strindberg's dialogue).

Less practicable was Strindberg's original idea of using a sciopticon, or
large magic lantern, to create back projections that would replace conventional painted scenery altogether. Although the experiments of the
playwright and his director succeeded in producing a large and distinct
image in the background, it proved necessary to keep the area in front
of the projection so dark that it became impossible to see the faces of the
actors clearly. The technological problem could not be solved, and eventually the experiments had to be abandoned. Instead, the traditionalist
designer Carl Grabow was called in to paint conventional perspective
backcloths to illustrate the shifting stations of the Unknown's symbolic
journey. The seventeen changes of scene in the play were, for the most
part, accomplished simply and swiftly by noiselessly lowering and raising Grabow's painted backcloths. To prevent any disruption of mood,
Strindberg wrote to Grandinson (October 25, 1900), these changes "must
take place in blackout, but without a curtain. As soon as the curtain comes
down, an audience gives itself a shake and rejects what it's seen!"

The representational but manifestly two-dimensional backdrops created by Grabow, on which furniture and other necessary items were
painted, corresponded perfectly to the kind of scenery which Strindberg

had denounced so vigorously in his Preface to *Miss Julie*. Now, however, his aim was not a sense of naturalistic illusion, but rather quite the opposite. Brecht once referred to the symbolist experiments of Maeterlinck and Strindberg as a form of Verfremdung – but this, too, is far from what Strindberg intended in *To Damascus*. His purpose is to "make strange" the events of the play, but not in order to render them subject to social criticism (as Brecht would want). Instead, the audience's comfortable sense of recognizable, everyday reality is disrupted in order to make the spectators aware of an unexpected metareality that underlies the life of all human beings. To make them "dreamers," as Bark says.

By causing Grabow's painted backdrops to be seen within the framework of the inner stage, in the subdued and impressionistic lighting of the coloured overhead projectors, a stylized effect was achieved that obliterated any sense of naturalistic solidity or sequentiality. The characters, one critic observed, seemed "to pop up and disappear as if by magic, thereby greatly strengthening the fantastical impression of these strange scenes."[6] The ephemeral, dreamlike quality of Grandinson's stage picture emerges even now in surviving rehearsal photographs of his production. In the opening scene, on the street corner where the Unknown first meets and follows the Lady, the director made some concession to a more realistic sense of three-dimensionality and depth: a corner of a small Gothic church, a café with its outdoor table and chairs, and a couple of other house facades were all suggested by free-standing flats. As the journey moved on, however, the staging grew simpler. For the encounter with the Physician, the werewolf–husband whom the Lady seeks to escape, Strindberg's rather elaborate description of the scene was reduced to a backcloth on which the three-sided courtyard with its towering wood-pile was painted. Here and in the interior scenes in the kitchen, the hotel room, and the Rose Chamber, a few pieces of furniture were placed in front of the backdrop. For the exterior scenes of the pilgrimage – on the highway, at the mountain pass, and by the sea – the raised inner stage remained completely bare, with the figures of the Unknown and the Lady outlined against the flat, painted background.

Rather different and more phantasmagorical in tone was the Asylum scene, the pivotal experience in the protagonist's ordeal. The entire action of the play is, in the last analysis, a projection of the fantasies, memories and dreams of the Unknown, but in the wholly hallucinatory Asylum episode he is brought face to face with a veritable chorus of doubles who represent "real" characters in his past life. To underscore the impression of the Unknown as the dreamer of this sequence, Grandinson carried

1   The Unknown (August Palme) questions the Abbess (Tyra Dörum) at the beginning of the Asylum scene. In this rehearsal photo from the world premiere of *To Damascus I* (Dramaten, 1900), the sinister "doubles" that the protagonist encounters are seated in an inner alcove created by the small vaulted arch in the picture. The second, larger arch used by Grandinson to frame the raised acting area itself is not visible here.

the metaphor of theatre-in-the-theatre one step further by establishing a yet smaller and more distanced inner stage. This recess was bathed in blue light and framed by a smaller vaulted arch that was a replica of the larger one he used to frame the raised acting area itself. Behind this inner opening, seated at a long refectory table that was illuminated in a ghostly green light, seventeen spectral, soup-eating emanations of the dreamer's guilt appeared before him – his grieving parents, a cruelly treated sister, an abandoned wife and children, the Lady, the threatening Physician and his madman (who bore an alarming resemblance to the dreamer), and others from his journey. The appearance of these "doubles" within the telescopic framework of the multiple arches created, as it were, a *mise-en-abîme* that further collapsed the difference between reality and dream. In this play, as in *A Dream Play*, the illusion of this difference deconstructs as the insistent correspondences between things emerge.

The horrors of the Asylum episode, from which the Unknown flees with the curses of Deuteronomy ringing in his ears, were effectively juxtaposed in Grandinson's production with beats of rest and quiet. The Unknown's reunion with the Lady ("By the Sea") in the fourth act was one such moment – "a scene of great tenderness, closeness, desperation, and love," as Ingmar Bergman has called it. In Bergman's production of the first two parts of the *Damascus* trilogy in 1974, this scene was played in a simple pool of light on an otherwise bare stage, using only a back projection of shining cloud formations that gradually took the form of shipmast crosses in its closing minutes. Although such was also the kind of solution Strindberg himself had envisioned, he was obliged to content himself with the style of staging depicted in one of the surviving rehearsal photographs from 1900, showing August Palme and Harriet Bosse standing hand in hand on the raised platform stage in front of Grabow's painted winter seascape. This photo, like the others from this production, fails to show the framing arch that effectively imparted both focus and distance to Grandinson's expressive figure compositions.

Although Grandinson was quite familiar with the symbolist experiments of Lugné-Poë and had even been instrumental in bringing the Parisian director and his troupe to Stockholm for guest performances in 1894, he and his actors wisely eschewed any trace of the intoned delivery and trance-like gestures of the symbolist school in their production of Strindberg's first dream play. Although the Swedish critics were somewhat divided in their opinion of August Palme's performance as the Unknown, it seems almost unreasonable to expect that the first actor to attempt this monumental role would be capable of mastering

2 This rehearsal photograph from the world premiere of *To Damascus I* shows the reunion of the Unknown and the Lady "by the sea," with Palme and Harriet Bosse standing hand in hand on the raised platform stage in front of Grabow's rather obviously painted seascape.

all of its complexities and contradictions. One of Palme's most memorable parts was Hjalmar Ekdal in Ibsen's *The Wild Duck*, and it seems (not unreasonably) to have been a touch of Hjalmar that he brought to Strindberg's dreamer – rich in lyrical warmth and conviviality, troubled by a nervous restlessness, but lacking the deep Strindbergian sense of suppressed suffering and anguish that the new challenge demanded. In his review in *Stockholms-Tidningen* (November 20, 1900) Alfred Lindkvist provided the most evocative description of the psychological intensity achieved in Palme's portrayal: "Marked by an artistic realism, his facial expression and pantomime revealed both the sombre melancholy of the thinker and the nervousness of the self-tormentor, agitated and strained to the point of madness. The haunted moods and fevered fantasies, the visions and premonitions that plague the penitent, all were delineated with compelling immediacy and intuitive strength."

"With all the conceitedness of youth, it seemed to me that acting had become stilted, declamatory, and false," Harriet Bosse later wrote of the period during which she joined the acting company at Dramaten, at the age of twenty-one.[7] Despite the self-effacing tone of her comment, Bosse was well aware that her understated, inward-looking performance style constituted a bold change in Swedish theatre – a change welcomed by Strindberg himself. After seeing her as Puck in *A Midsummer-Night's Dream*, the role in which she first attracted critical attention earlier that season, he personally gave her the part of the Lady under whose spell the Unknown falls in *To Damascus*. The playwright himself, for whom life, dream, and drama were inextricably bound up, quickly fell under a comparable spell; six months later Harriet Bosse became his third wife. Apart from the personal side of the story, however, it becomes clear that Strindberg recognized in Bosse a new kind of actor whose quiet, allusive style corresponded perfectly to the associational, mutational dramaturgy of his dream plays. Most of the reviewers agreed that she played the Lady "simply, naturally, quietly, and with an irresistibly poignant appeal" (*Aftonbladet*). Tor Hedberg (*Svenska Dagbladet*) found that Bosse and Axel Hansson, who played the Physician, were the two actors who "understood best how to accommodate themselves to the play's strange quality of half-reality, half-unreality." Many of the critics' objections to Bosse's playing style focused on the fact that her extreme restraint often conveyed the impression of inexpressiveness and lack of vitality. A whiff of this criticism is evident even in the note Strindberg sent to her after the emotionally charged dress rehearsal that had been held on the day of the opening: "It was great and beautiful (Damascus), although

I had imagined the character somewhat lighter, with little touches of mischief and with more expansiveness. A little of Puck – these were my first words to you and will be my last! A smile in the midst of misery suggests the existence of hope, and the situation doesn't turn out to be hopeless after all!" (November 19, 1900).

Harriet Bosse's unconventionally introspective and understated interpretation of the Lady was thus another of the key elements that made the world premiere of *To Damascus I* such a pivotal event. Grandinson's carefully rehearsed mise-en-scène gave audiences their first convincing demonstration of the inherent performability of the post-Inferno plays. In the process, it transported Strindberg out of the nineteenth century and into the twentieth, squarely at the forefront of developments in modernist theatre. The essence of Grandinson's keen responsiveness to Strindberg's new genre was sensitivity to the inner, associational rhythm that governs his form – which, as Kandinsky later reminds us, is itself "the outer expression of the inner content." In this respect, the performance of a play like *To Damascus* is its meaning, what it is about. In a later essay that compares reading Strindberg with seeing him performed, Grandinson observes that at early rehearsals of a Strindberg play, he frequently found that "lines, situations acquire a value when spoken or shown in action that is completely different from that which anyone who only reads the play could ever expect."[8]

On the other hand, Hedberg spoke for many when he declared in his review that *To Damascus* "certainly has a stronger impact on the reader than on the theatre spectator; its sombre and fragmented fantasies cannot always stand to be embodied" in performance. To prove him wrong, new theatrical techniques had to be found, capable of better articulating the complexities of Strindberg's dramatic expressionism on the stage. It is to Grandinson's credit that he pointed the way while having virtually none of these techniques at his disposal.

STRINDBERG AND THE NEW STAGECRAFT

"The modern stage is a sorcerer's box full of a thousand possibilities, and we make a mistake if we do not use them," Pär Lagerkvist proclaimed in *Modern Theatre: Points of View and Attack*, a seminal reassessment of Strindberg's stature and significance that appeared six years after the playwright's death in 1912.[9] In his ringing repudiation of naturalism, Lagerkvist sees Strindberg as the true source of "the renewal of the modern drama, and thereby also the gradual renewal of the theatre. It is from him and through him that naturalism received the critical blow even if, moreover, it is also Strindberg who gave naturalism its most dramatic works. If one wishes to understand the direction in which the modern theatre is actually striving, and the line of development it will probably follow, it is certainly wise to turn to him first of all" (20). As this spokesman for a new generation contends, the complex spatial and temporal dynamics of Strindberg's post-Inferno dramas could not be adequately realized in performance until the more modern techniques of a new stagecraft – the cyclorama, advanced methods of lighting and back projections, and not least the revolving stage – were introduced. Once these advances became a reality, however, the full range of this writer's dramatic oeuvre, from the earliest works of the romantic period to the post-Inferno plays, were taken up for reconsideration and revival by a generation of younger theatre artists eager for a theatrical revolution. Ringing in their ears was Lagerkvist's affirmation of Strindberg's "newly created dramatic form" as the quintessence of the artistic instinct of the new age.

Although *A Dream Play* and *The Ghost Sonata* were more central to the new theatre movement that Lagerkvist's manifesto invokes, the widely influential Berlin premiere of *To Damascus I* was the event that inaugurated a veritable wave of experimental German performances of the post-Inferno plays. Victor Barnowsky, who had succeeded Otto Brahm as head of the respected Lessing Theatre the previous year, directed this production. By far its most distinctive feature was the authoritative characterization of the Unknown created by Friedrich Kayssler. As a director, Kayssler was becoming a leading force in the expressionistic movement that swept across Germany at this time. An imposing and profoundly soulful figure as an actor, his portrayal of the Unknown conveyed the deeply human sense of suffering and guilt that some critics had found wanting in Palme's earlier interpretation. In this case the actor's touchstone, so to speak, was not the character of Hjalmar Ekdal but that of Faust – the role Kayssler had played for Max Reinhardt both in his productions of Part I (1909) and Part II (1911). *Faust II* in particular, with its dramatization of the search for spiritual fulfilment and its related emphasis on the elements of dream and fantasy, seemed to represent an obvious analogue to Strindberg's *Damascus* trilogy. Kayssler's Unknown was thus very grand and spiritual – too much so for Alfred Polgar, a staunch champion of Brahm's naturalistic Ibsen productions who objected that the actor's tone of defiant melancholy was monotonous and tended at times toward chanted litany.[10] In a later program article published in

1920, Kayssler himself offers the critical opinion that the other characters in the play such as the Physician, the Madman, the Mother, and the
Old Man are not "real" at all, but are rather self-invented instruments
of punishment which the guilty soul of the Unknown projects upon the
surface of the external world.[11]

The critics described Kayssler's encounters with these figures in the
Barnowsky production with such words as "fantastical and hallucinatory" (*Berliner Zeitung am Mittag*, April 18, 1914). With its eerie music,
shadowy darkness, and ghost-like figures, the Asylum scene in particular
impressed the seasoned playgoer Siegfried Jacobsohn as "a shadow play,
in which there was not the risk of even an instant of boredom."[12] "In
ghostly fashion the stage pictures rush by," another reviewer wrote when
the production reached Vienna a month after its Berlin opening. "It continually seems as though the characters are not moving on solid ground"
(*Neue Freie Presse*, May 19, 1914). It seems, however, that the smoothness of
"the oscillation between dream and waking, between reality and vision"
so admired by this observer had not been achieved without considerable early difficulties. Despite the use of a revolving stage, the bulky
modernist scenery designed by the cosmopolitan Danish scenographer
Svend Gade inflicted protracted delays on the long performance, causing more than one of the critics to hark back fondly to the simplicity
of Grandinson's approach fourteen years before.[13] Gade's complicated
scene changes compelled Barnowsky to lower a black curtain after each
and every episode. For the same reason, the text itself eventually had to
be stripped to thirteen scenes (by cutting two pairs of episodes, in the
hotel room and at the mountain pass) in order to produce the desired
impression on an audience of "swiftly changing, lightly stylized pictures
on the turning stage" (*Berliner Tageblatt*, April 18, 1914).

The Strindberg renaissance that continued to flourish in Germany
throughout the turbulent years of the First World War made its impact
on Scandinavian theatre chiefly through the touring productions of Max
Reinhardt. The smoothly coordinated Reinhardt ensemble opened the
eyes of Swedish audiences to the musical, visionary power of Strindberg's
late plays with their expressionistic performances of *The Ghost Sonata* in
1917 and *The Pelican* [*Pelikanen*] three years later. By then, however, the
versatile young Swedish director Per Lindberg, who had studied under
Reinhardt during the war, had already begun to put into practice the
modernist aims and techniques he had absorbed during his Berlin apprenticeship. With his appointment in 1918 to the newly built Lorensberg
Theatre in Gothenburg, Lindberg had at his disposal an ultramodern

technical facility, incorporating a cyclorama, a revolving stage, and a highly advanced lighting board capable of realizing his objective of "lighting as mise-en-scène" rather than as simple illumination. As one of the brightest and most dedicated advocates of the New Stagecraft, Lindberg's avowed purpose at the Lorensberg was the creation of a new, non-illusionistic scenic art devoted to "expression rather than decoration"(*Göteborgs-Posten*, March 30, 1918). His artistic collaborator during his years in Gothenburg was Knut Ström, a stage designer who had worked for six years at the avant-garde Schauspielhaus in Düsseldorf and thus fully shared Lindberg's view of the stage as "a place only for bodies and levels, not for painted exteriors."[14] An architectural rather than a painted stage, rhythmic linear movement, plastic statuesqueness, and a musical harmony of colours – these were for Lindberg and Ström, as they were for the other adherents of the New Stagecraft, the basic ingredients of modern theatrical art.

Within the simplified, stylized, and suggestive theatrical context advocated by these reformers, Strindberg's poetic imagination could achieve virtually free rein. Before turning his attention to an overtly expressionistic work such as *To Damascus*, however, Lindberg first applied his method to two of Strindberg's most popular historical dramas, each of which had enjoyed a successful stage life in the naturalistic vein during the dramatist's lifetime. Early in 1920 he staged the verse version of *Master Olof*, including for the first time Strindberg's bitter metatheatrical "afterpiece" depicting "the creation of the world and its true meaning." The Lindberg production was as revolutionary in spirit as Strindberg's own defiantly revisionist view of the familiar figures and events of his country's history. The history-play conventions of "accurate" architecture and "authentic" interiors and accessories were conclusively set aside, and the strict simplicity of Ström's scenography and costumes set a new example whose influence would continue to be felt for decades to come. "What can and is to be included of the historical milieu" wrote art historian Axel Romdahl in *Svenska Dagbladet* (January 21, 1920), "is decided solely according to the principle that nothing unnecessary must be shown, nothing false must be shown, and that, if anything beyond the unavoidable is shown, this must have a suggestive weight capable of underscoring and emphasizing the dramatic action." This elimination of naturalistic detail served to focus attention instead on the inner drama of the vacillating protagonist, the hyperreflective religious revolutionary Olaus Petri (Master Olof) who betrays himself when he becomes a tool for other men's purposes.

Although inspired in formal terms by the Shakespearean model, Strindberg's concept of the history play is very much his own, shaped by his conviction that in dramatizing history "the purely human is of major interest, and history the background; the inner struggles of souls awaken more sympathy than the combat of soldiers and the storming of walls" (*LIT*, 266). One of the most compelling examples of this Strindbergian tension between the inner action of suffering and the outer action of spectacle is *The Saga of the Folkungs* [*Folkungssagan*], which he completed at about the same time as *To Damascus I* and which came to the stage in full naturalistic regalia in 1901. On a superficial level, the play is a sweeping historical chronicle of the problems of a weak king in a turbulent and rebellious time. (Strindberg himself draws a parallel to Shakespeare's dramatization of the War of the Roses.) On a deeper symbolic level, however, King Magnus, the last of the Folkungs, is the passive sacrificial victim of the grim, retributive force we call history (or the Eternal One), doomed to expiate an ancient ancestral crime, suffering perhaps in order to purge his society of its evil (symbolized in the apocalyptic plague scene that surely must have been Ingmar Bergman's inspiration for the comparable scene in his film *The Seventh Seal*). This inner action of suffering and expiation was doubtless what drew Lindberg to the play, which he directed at the Lorensberg less than ten months after his *Master Olof*. This time he used an even more radically stylized Ström setting to detach the play conclusively from the conventions of historical authenticity. His raked, checkerboard stage was an asymmetrical, consciously naïve rendering of a Serlio-style city square, intended to evoke the sense of a sixteenth-century woodcut – a pastiche of a period, in other words, rather than a reproduction of it. Lindberg's expressive stage pictures were "painted" entirely with light, colour, and vivid figure compositions. The first of the mass scenes in the square, when Magnus is hailed by the jubilant multitude, seemed to Stockholm critic August Brunius (*Svenska Dagbladet*, November 21, 1920) "quite simply without parallel."

We have never seen anything as magnificent on a Swedish stage as this immense altarpiece, in which every figure stands in clear, sculptural plasticity, wrapped in a dreamy mist and etched against a storm-blue horizon. Its beauty culminates in the Madwoman's silhouette against the sky – a Giotto fantasy as riveting for the eye as for the mind, equally powerful as a picture and a dramatic revelation.

In their radically antinaturalistic style and untraditional approach, Lindberg's two productions of the history plays paralleled and actually anticipated one of the most challenging of the New Stagecraft experiments in Strindberg – Evgeny Vakhtangov's theatricalist rendering of *Erik XIV* at the First Studio of the Moscow Art Theatre in March of 1921. Vakhtangov conceived his performance ("more like a futurist fantasy than a history play," Lindberg later thought when he saw it in 1927) as a pro-Bolshevik denunciation of the "contradictory royal power" that inevitably dooms the sensitive, ineffectual protagonist, played as the tragic victim of his destiny by the renowned Russian actor Michael Chekhov. The mise-en-scène delineated a double perspective, a juxtaposition of two conflicting worlds and styles. In the midst of the robust, realistically depicted world of the common people lay the masked, moribund prison-world of Erik's court, defined by crumbling pillars and labyrinthine passageways, grotesque gestures and movements, and expressionistic signifiers of impending disaster. ("Arrows in the crown, arrows on the sword, arrows on the costumes, on the faces, on the walls," the director wrote.) At the core of Vakhtangov's boldly experimental performance was, in fact, the same adamant rejection of the naturalistic concept of realistic illusion that had likewise come to inspire Strindberg in his post-Inferno period. The Russian director had even considered creating a prologue for *Erik XIV* to remind his audience that they are watching a performance, not eavesdropping on life: "We should do away with the need for the audience to peep from behind the corner. The audience should constantly feel itself in the theatre, not guests at Uncle Vanya's," Vakhtangov insisted. "Theatre should always be theatre."[15]

Even more acutely expressionistic than Vakhtangov's *Erik XIV*, however, was the staging of the Scandinavian premiere of *To Damascus III* at the Lorensberg Theatre in 1922. Directed by Knut Ström and designed by him and his apprentice Sandro Malmquist, this skilfully condensed version of Part III presented the final stations of the Unknown's pilgrimage on a virtually empty stage. Alone its sheer bareness evoked a powerful sense of great height and space that emphasized the existential isolation and bewilderment of Strindberg's modern Everyman. Ström's sketch for an abstract mountain landscape is an imaginative collage of skewed horizontal planes, raked inclines, and geometrical forms. Within this "rhythmic space" (as Appia might have called it) all recourse to figurative representation was eschewed; instead, Malmquist introduced projections of significant objects or shapes on the cyclorama – the silhouette of a signpost outlined against the sky, for instance – that took the place of constructed scenery.

Less than four years later, during an extraordinary season of plays which he directed at the newly built Concert Hall in Stockholm in

3 A purely expressionistic design by Knut Ström for his production of *To Damascus III* at the Lorensberg Theatre in Gothenburg in 1922.

1926/7, Lindberg himself turned his attention to the final movement of the *Damascus* trilogy. This time the venue was the formal, curtainless platform of the concert hall itself – an open stage that corresponded perfectly, in Lindberg's view, to "the expressionistic vision of theatrical space as a unified whole . . . a flexible space in which stage arrangement, actors, and audience, unified by the architecture of the place, share a common rhythm and emotion."[16] A purely expressionistic setting by John Jon-And conveyed a stylized impression of a mountain landscape made up of angular, abstract planes and contours. The dominant shape of a strangely distorted cross appeared to signify the monastery refuge where the Unknown hopes at last to find escape from the world of unreason and deceit. Although Harriet Bosse, Strindberg's model for the role, played the character of the Lady, the evening's strongest performance came from the noted Norwegian actor Ingolf Schanche, whose ironical portrayal of the Tempter stole the spotlight (something that the Unknown's talkative Mephisphelean sidekick is apt to do in this play).

Schanche's mocking and expressive countenance and his ability to combine irony and dread in his interpretations made him an ideal Strindberg actor. As such, he was the obvious choice for the part of the

Unknown when Lindberg subsequently directed a one-evening adaptation of all three parts of *To Damascus* at Nationaltheatret in Oslo in 1933. During the war years in Germany, both Kayssler and Barnowsky had staged two-evening productions of the trilogy (Part I on the first night, a condensation of Parts II and III on the second). Lindberg was evidently the first director to attempt a shortened version of all three parts on a single night – and the distinguished Norwegian critic Kristian Elster was the first but not the last to object to such an amalgamation. "The three plays are neither interconnected nor continuous actions," Elster argued in his review. "They are three variations on the same theme. They are three plays that can be performed individually, but when performed together they must all three be butchered. The plays are different in tone and in style." Despite the textual objections to which this critic points, however, he was by no means blind to the great emotional force of Schanche's performance. "With an inner absorption in the role, a human understanding of it, a surrender to the experience of it" he struggled with what Elster calls "feverish virtuosity" to make emotional sense of the contradictory protagonist at the centre of Lindberg's problematic experiment.[17] One of the moments in which Lindberg's vivid mise-en-scène and Schanche's ironic attack formed a perfect union was the overtly expressionistic sequence near the end of Part II, known as the Goldmaker's Banquet. "I have seldom seen anything as fascinating on a stage as this open, dream-slow transformation, in darkness pierced by flickering shafts of light," wrote the Swedish reviewer Herbert Grevenius:

From the banquet scene with its stiff, formal attire [we were transposed] to the tavern table, with slinking hooligans and hideous women all engaged in hushed and very intense whispering that seemed to come from all corners of the stage, and with Schanche standing motionless by the edge of his table, eyes closed with one hand to his neck, speaking and answering as if in a hypnotic trance. And then suddenly a change to violet, as a transition to a vision of sea and eternally fading horizon.[18]

This scene is a textbook example of the use of expressionism in the theatre, which allows the spectator to view events on stage through the distorted and fevered perspective of the protagonist-dreamer, who in this case finds that what he had imagined to be an elegant testimonial banquet to honour "the Great Goldmaker" has now somehow changed in an instant to a shabby and hostile collection of ruffians in a cheap café. In his writings Lindberg uses the term "expressionism" very loosely, as a way of describing the work of almost every theatre modernist from Craig and Appia to Meyerhold and even Jacques Copeau. He is more precise, however, when he characterizes what he regards as the expressionistic style of Strindberg's dream plays and chamber plays. In none of these, he argues, is there "any gallery of psychologically motivated characters whose comings and goings are carefully explained."

Nor are different sides of the author objectified in the form of various "characters." The protagonist is the Unknown, the Poet, the Stranger, the Man, a wanderer, an observer, a seeker, a penitent, without "ideals" but with great passion. A spiritual centre. And the figures around him are grotesque projections of elements of the protagonist's soul, symbolic emanations of the life of his imagination, reflected images of the drama's central ego. Naturally they have no personal names. Hovering about the Unknown like broken shadows are the the the Confessor, the Physician, the Beggar, Caesar the Madman – they merge one into another; the one knows what the other has thought and said; they could as well be one and the same person. Such is the skeletal form of these plays, and such became the skeletal form of the expressionistic drama.[19]

THE MOLANDER ALTERNATIVE

Although neither Lindberg nor his great model Max Reinhardt were narrowly or rigidly expressionistic in their Strindberg productions, the sweeping revolution in Strindberg interpretation that occurred in the mid-1930s in Sweden took as its point of departure the repudiation of all expressionism as a key to understanding the deeper meaning of the post-Inferno plays. The intellectual architect of the new movement was Martin Lamm, whose criticism strove to emphasize the rootedness of these plays in the concrete reality of the dramatist's own life experiences. The dream episodes in a work like *To Damascus* are, Lamm argues, not meant to be "contrived terror scenes arranged through the dexterity of a clever director"; rather, these moments must be "experienced just like the everyday events in his dramas."[20] In the succession of productions staged by Olof Molander in the thirties and after, Lamm's ideas came to play an important part in the shaping of a new style of performance that restored to Strindberg's plays a relevance and a Swedishness that conclusively set aside the approach taken by Reinhardt and his followers. Molander's seminal revivals were imaginative in their application of the modernist principles of the New Stagecraft yet solidly grounded in the concrete milieu and tone of Strindberg's Stockholm. To most observers, their fluid, supple scenic form seemed more responsive than ever before to the associational, metamorphic nature of Strindberg's dramatic logic. As a young man Molander had been deeply impressed by Reinhardt's visiting production of *The Pelican* in 1920, calling it "a scenic masterpiece that is not even suggested by a reading of that chamber play."[21] Eventually, however, he came to regard "the German, Reinhardt-inspired romantic expressionism" manifested by this production as "completely alien to Strindberg's surrealistic, dream-play dramaturgy. It is certainly true that nightmares are often its subject, but nightmares of everyday, of life as we live it, not a nightmare existence in any higher sense, not a caricature."[22]

In 1937, during the season after his first, epoch-making production of *A Dream Play*, Molander chose to mark the twenty-fifth anniversary of Strindberg's death with a revival of *To Damascus I* at Dramaten, where it had not been played since Grandinson's world premiere of the play. The backbone of this startling performance was its director's avowed intention to stress "the autobiographical and the religious elements" in the drama. "For the Unknown in this play is, to some extent, Strindberg himself" (*Stockholms Tidningen*, February 26, 1937). Lars Hanson, one of his country's foremost Strindberg actors, was costumed and made up to convey a distinct resemblance to the playwright himself. His very personal, unhistrionic reading of the main character captured the difficult mixture of tragic anguish and arch irony in the play and its nameless protagonist. "With an intuition that is quite unique," wrote Sten Selander in *Svenska Dagbladet* (February 28), "Lars Hanson has grasped and has allowed his infinitely revealing face to express what in some ways lies hidden at the very core of this role – a small, frightened, helpless young man with a guilty conscience, unable even to comprehend why he is buffeted so hard by Fate." In turn, this sense of incomprehension established a more complex ironic perspective that often made the Unknown seem the bewildered spectator of his own life-dream. He succeeded in making the character "not only humanly believable but also humanly appealing," Agne Beijer observed in a brilliant essay on this production (published first as a review in *Göteborgs Handels- och Sjöfartstidningen*, March 1-2, 1937). Although Sweden's foremost theatre researcher expressed doubt about the general soundness of Lamm's method of explicating a literary work on the basis of the identification of the autobiographical events underlying it, he had only praise for the end result reached by Lars Hanson in performance. "He left Strindberg out of it and made the role live its own life . . . One had the impression of a personal identification with the role that actually circumvents analysis, even though the characterization was, beyond any doubt, the product of an analysis that was, in its own way, no less penetrating or less precise than the research of literary criticism."[23]

4 Work photograph of the setting by Sven-Erik Skawonius for the opening scene on the street corner in Molander's 1937 production of *To Damascus I*. The downspout to the right of the café, a fragment of the church portal to the left, and the narrow "road" of paving stones running across the forestage were retained in Skawonius' scenography as framing elements in subsequent scenes.

As a devoted disciple of Gordon Craig, Molander was convinced that the modern stage "must not represent reality, it must bring forth an image of it, it must conjure up reality. When our imagination is activated by what we see on the stage, we boldly create a reality far more real than what can ever be represented on any stage."[24] In his new mise-en-scène for *To Damascus*, however, he strenuously avoided the abstract, non-representational quality that often characterized Lindberg's productions of Strindberg. "Molander has not attempted anything eccentric, and he seems in general to have been determined not to allow the visual element to intrude too much upon us and obscure the inner action," Beijer remarked. He describes the settings designed by Sven-Erik Skawonius as "naturalistically constructed but at the same time imbued with the drama's special mood to such an extent that the air of half-reality intended by Strindberg is just as fully achieved."[25] With "its bizarre dream contour, its almost unreal light" (*Aftonbladet*), the Molander–Skawonius scenography thus achieved a surreal doubleness, in which tangible, recognizable reality was collapsed into the steadily more insistent presence of an oneiric shadow-world.

At the outset, for the street-corner scene where the Unknown's journey begins (and ends), Skawonius created a solid, sharply lifelike setting that seemed to hark back to the days of Grabow and Grandinson. Yet even here there was something unsettling behind the lifelikeness. "The ghostly mood could be found," Nils Beyer observed, "already from the moment the curtain rose on the street corner with its dead house, its Gothic gateway, and that pitch-black alley where all the world's misfortunes seemed to lurk" (*Social-Demokraten*, February 28, 1937). At the end of the scene, after Maria Ekström's gentle, very maternal Lady impulsively kissed the Unknown and he followed her out, the "real" world of the street corner disappeared as their shadowy dream-journey began. In the Molander production, however, deconstructed fragments of this reality – a corner of the Gothic church stage right and a corresponding bit of a house façade with a downspout on the opposite side – remained visible (with greater or lesser prominence) throughout the ensuing scenes of the pilgrimage. The sides of the frame created by these permanent iconic flats were connected by a stylized "road" of paving stones that ran the width of the shallow forestage, one step below the level of the actual stage itself. The result – clearly visible in, for example, the photograph of Skawonius' stark setting for the wintry reunion of the lovers by the sea – was the creation of a window effect, framing and distancing the scene in a manner that heightened its dreamlike quality. (Grandinson, it

5 In this photograph of the stark, wintry setting created by Skawonius for the reunion of the Unknown and the Lady by the sea, the framing elements from the opening scene – the downspout at the right, a glimpse of the church wall at the left, and the paved road across the front – are clearly visible.

will be remembered, had achieved an analogous effect by rather different means, using a vaulted, curtainless arch to demarcate a raised inner stage on which all seventeen of the play's episodes were acted, including the opening and closing scenes.)

The scenography created by Molander and Skawonius for *To Damascus* depended on the deft intermingling of back projections and bits and pieces of actual scenery. The Physician's veranda, for example, was basically a large folding screen perforated with windowpanes of strangely coloured glass, situated in what appeared to be a black, mountainous void. By contrast, the setting for the pivotal Asylum scene consisted only of a towering projection of a vast, shadowy cathedral interior, supplemented by a somewhat fuller glimpse of the omnipresent street-corner church and its steps at one side. Bathed in eerie green light, the accusing "doubles" sat like a coroner's jury at a long table in the background as Lars Hanson, seated apart at a smaller table and dressed in a long,

cassock-like robe, registered the effects of the Confessor's litany of curses
on his horrified Strindberg countenance. The exterior stations on the
journey were much more simplified – barren, cheerless landscapes where
Beckett could suitably be performed. At the stopping place called On
the Highway, where Strindberg envisioned rolling hills, lush vegetation,
and a picturesque grove of "shrines and Alpine crosses," the wanderers
in Molander's production found only an empty, hilly wasteland, broken
by a roadside shrine and crucifix on which the Saviour hung facing away
from them. The only other object in sight was Strindberg's ironic plac-
ard prohibiting vagrancy. Both the second scene at the shrine and the
ensuing replay of By the Sea were depicted in the grip of bitter winter
cold. Skawonius' setting for the latter episode, consisting of a rustic bench
against an abstract background of similarly hilly topography, was overshadowed by a projection of winter clouds and the spectral image of the
masts of the wrecked ship (which the Unknown instantly misinterprets as
crosses signifying some "new Golgotha" of suffering that perhaps awaits
him and his companion.)

These latter scenes, which "blow toward you like an icy blast of loneliness and profound cold," were ultimately counterbalanced in the last
scene by what Grevenius called "the contrasting depth and warmth of
the glow" projected by the rosette window of the church on the corner (*Stockholms Tidningen*, February 28). Strindberg's final point is not, of
course, "redemption" in any orthodox sense, for as he himself pointed
out in his early letter to Geijerstam, the pilgrimage "begins again at the
same point as the action stops." The struggle with the Unseen One is
never finished; it merely reconstitutes itself in a new guise. Thus, the
ironic open conclusion reached by Molander's production was simply
that, as Grevenius puts it, "when the light finally dies away and the curtain
falls, the street corner now seems almost kindly in its Sunday-afternoon
melancholy."

Molander was an extremely versatile director whose style, even within
the Strindberg repertory, was by no means limited to the radical simplification and oneiric introspection of his interpretations of *A Dream Play* and
To Damascus. Barely ten months after the latter production, he undertook
his third major excursion into the post-Inferno period with his staging of
The Saga of the Folkungs, an ambitious experiment bursting with theatrical pageantry conceived on a colossal scale. Not unlike Lindberg's initial
revival of this work seventeen years earlier, the Molander–Skawonius version of it was essentially a rich medieval tapestry of choreographed mass
scenes and spectacular visual effects. Although Beijer and other critics

expressed reservations about the interpretation of the play as simple historical extravaganza, Grevenius' vivid account in *Stockholms Tidningen* (October 23, 1937) suggests the powerful sensual impact achieved by Molander's grandiose mise-en-scène:

A gallows stands like a grim pointer toward eternity, and an immense iron chain stretches a meaningful greeting from a distant heaven to a desperate earth. Grotesque tumult and ceremonies, royal splendour and rage, drunken torchlight processions, Dominicans and Franciscans with flaming candles, the fever-red Plague Girl whirling about with her broom and chalking her crosses [on the doors of the doomed], the frenzied monotonous dancing of the flagellants, with blood streaming down their backs, King Magnus groaning beneath his black penitential cross, the Madwoman on the roof shouting out: "There is blood on your crown, King Magnus." One is caught in the grip of these intense visual pictures.

During the following decades, Molander went on to direct many other important Strindberg revivals, including *The Ghost Sonata* in 1942, *To Damascus II* two years later, *The Great Highway* [*Stora landsvägen*] in 1949, and others. In 1965, the year before his death, he returned once more to the *Damascus* challenge, this time with a production of all three parts of the cycle on the small studio stage of the Stockholm City Theatre. Like Lindberg's single-evening presentation of the trilogy in Oslo twenty-two years earlier, Molander's chamber-theatre version sought to convey a sustaining internal unity that, in the opinion of most Strindberg scholars, is not to be found in the texts themselves. His austere distillation was, however, a radical departure not only from Lindberg's style but also from his own previous practice. "All in the *Damascus* trilogy that is nightmare, ghostly vision, hallucination, and symbolism has been cleansed away with astringent intellectual acid, and lingering reminiscences that remain seem out of place or even incomprehensible," Per Erik Wahlund wrote in *Svenska Dagbladet* (May 15, 1965). A moment of theatrical spectacle such as the Goldmaker's Banquet was deliberately reduced to an expressionistic projection and the sound of voices on the P.A. system. The stage was completely bare throughout, except for three benchlike shapes; the thirty-three scene "changes" in Molander's adaptation were indicated only by the allusive projections of Per Falk, a large number of which were non-figurative.

The end result of the experiment was a "didactic and dialectical chamber play" that seemed intended, in Wahlund's view, to illustrate Martin Lamm's observation about the *Damascus* trilogy: "The struggle is waged not between the Unknown and the other characters but between him and the Unseen One, who from beyond the stage rains down blows on the protagonist and finally wins the battle."[26] Within the tight confines of Molander's detheatricalized mise-en-scène, however, this struggle became more an intellectual process than an emotional or spiritual ordeal. The acting style in the performance was fully as restrained and understated as its staging. Keve Hjelm played the Unknown virtually without make-up, in a costume that alluded to photographs of Strindberg at the turn of the century. Here, however, any resemblance to a tormented genius ended. "Although we would never mistake him for a great poet – and such was surely never Molander's plan – we still find ourselves brought face to face with an intelligent and basically religious neurasthenic," Wahlund observed. "Despite – or perhaps because of – the lowering of the emotional level, this rebel and raisonneur displays, above all, intellectual honesty." Even Toivo Pawlo's suavely diabolical Tempter ("at once both threatening and sociable, dangerous and appealing") shared Hjelm's low-keyed, cerebral approach. In general, however, the conscious intellectual subversion of the emotional intensity of *To Damascus* in this production did nothing to make the play more accessible to a contemporary audience. For, as Molander himself had demonstrated in earlier productions of the dream plays, only through a direct appeal to its intuitive emotional responsiveness can a theatre audience be induced to embrace the strange half-reality of Strindberg's allusive dramatic action.

In retrospect, Molander's most fundamental contribution to the understanding of Strindberg's later plays was surely his grasp of their inherent theatricality. The commingling of the real and the phantasmagorical in his best productions – call it surrealism or "fantastic realism" or what you will – was not a directorial concept imposed on a given text but a carefully scored theatrical transcription of its inner dramaturgical rhythm. "At first, Strindberg's inferno dramas put the strangest visions into the heads of Europe's directors, who . . . began to throw themselves into levels, projections, and other devices for all they were worth," Ingmar Bergman wrote in a program article that accompanied his first professional Strindberg production, a revival of *The Pelican* on the intimate studio stage of the Malmö City Theatre in 1945.

It was director's theatre, display theatre, but it wasn't Strindberg. Molander has made us see the magic in Strindberg's dramaturgy. We have begun to understand that the strange fascination of the stage itself and the Strindbergian dialogue are compatible. Molander gives us Strindberg without embellishments or directorial visions, tunes in to the text, and leaves it at that. He makes us hear the poet's anxiety-driven fever pulse. It becomes an image of toiling, weeping, evil-smitten humanity. We listen to a strange, muted chamber music. And the dream play emerges in all its grotesqueness, its terror, and its beauty . . . I want only to express my debt of gratitude to Molander.[27]

This descriptive homage to Molander and his style bears witness to Bergman's awareness – reiterated many times since – of the formative influence exerted by this style on his own work with Strindberg. Yet despite the Molander "reminiscences" that occur, especially in Bergman's earlier productions, the character of this influence is by no means unambiguous. Particularly in Bergman's productions of post-Inferno plays at Dramaten over the past thirty years, both the elaborate visual effects and the biographical and religious symbolism associated with the Molander tradition have been expunged in his quest for a new kind of "reality" in the theatre, rooted solely in the direct and unimpeded confrontation between the audience and the living actor.

SCENES FROM A MARRIAGE

"After reading through *Damascus* again, it seems to me that the 2 parts with cuts could both be presented in the same evening between 7 and 11," Strindberg wrote to Geijerstam in the same letter (October 17, 1898) in which he had suggested using scenery "in an abstract, shadow-like, colourless tone." Bergman's production of the first two parts of the *Damascus* trilogy, which opened at Dramaten to a tumultuous reception early in 1974, was the first practical response to the playwright's suggestion. While faithfully mirroring the sequential logic and flow of the original, this reorchestration infused the first two parts of *To Damascus* with a new sense of coherence and organic interrelatedness. Those critics who objected to the disruption of Strindberg's satisfyingly symmetrical design in Part I were evidently overlooking the fact that an analogous and no less deliberate formal design governed Bergman's repatterning. Although two pairs of short scenes – in the hotel room and at the mountain pass – were eliminated in his version, the centrality of the Unknown's unnerving experience in the asylum was still manifestly emphasized in his rearrangement of the incidents. Following this episode, the protagonist retraced his steps exactly. Four scenes later, he was reunited with the Lady at the very spot – by the sea – where they had begun their wearisome journey as man and wife, after leaving the home of the Lady's former husband, the Physician. Part II thus emerged as the direct, infernal consequence of this reunion. "I have at all times seen the second part as the

depths of hell. Just as in a spiral, one sinks ever deeper, at last giving up
the struggle and going over to religion, to the church," reads part of a
note in the director's script. Given this clue, it is not difficult to discern
the logic of Bergman's decision to eliminate the final three scenes of Part I
and proceed, with the film maker's sense of an effective cut, directly to
the much more harrowing domestic and emotional conflicts that culmi-
nate in that appalling ritual of humiliation known as the Goldmaker's
Banquet. "The effect is so strong and the decision so obvious that we only
ask ourselves why it had never been done before," Alf Thoor declared in
Expressen (February 2, 1974). "For here we have a pattern that is eternal,
a structure that will never weaken. It begins with their marriage. It ends
with their parting. 'Scenes from a Marriage' would not have been a bad
subtitle for *To Damascus* in this interpretation."

Each individual scene in this production stood out with sculptural clarity, like a figure cluster on an ancient frieze or vase. One distinct group of
scenes were "close-ups" very tightly focused within the prescribed limits
of a raised, rectangular platform placed at the front edge of the stage.
"Settings" consisted only of back projections, a screen or two (often to
facilitate entrances or exits), and the barest minimum of furniture. The
spurious realism of a physical setting that purports to be a facsimile of
life has held no interest for Bergman as a stage director. "Once you
agree that the only important things are the words, the actors, and the
audience, then it isn't the setting that matters," he has repeatedly maintained. Even Strindberg himself, in his capacity as director of the Intimate
Theatre, would doubtless have approved the memorandum found at the
beginning of Bergman's script, titled simply "Technical Solution":

It is always best if one uses for the setting nothing other than lighting, which
always indicates the distribution [of scenes]. But I cannot do that here, where
all sorts of things have to be shown and must appear and disappear. Therefore I
see that we must avail ourselves of our stage platform and a few precise elements
and pictures and *four young men who will sit on the stage throughout* and will carry
things in and out . . . Then, the problems are eliminated. All the things are there,
standing right there from the beginning.

The scheme of visual presentation described in this memorandum
is intimately related to the director's concept of the mutational dream
rhythm of *To Damascus*. The scenography, Thoor observed in his review,
consisted "of some few, easily portable things that are carried in and out
swiftly and noiselessly – here a screen, there a sofa – together with projections on a black wall. In the nightmare scenes, the background is suddenly

and silently drawn aloft to reveal a ghostly banquet or a wretched bar-room on the outskirts of hell. And then, gone again. Completely without effort, one scene glides into the next in a matter of two or three seconds." A complex collage of giant back projections, designed by Marik Vos, con-sisted for the most part of stylized white-on-black drawings projected on the cyclorama or on a high screen positioned in the middle of the stage. The one other significant detail to which the memorandum makes ref-erence is the low "stage platform" that – as in many other Bergman productions – established the requisite point of focus and concentrated energy in his stage space. Utterly unlike the framed, distanced effect imparted to this play's scenes by the Grandinson–Molander approach, Bergman's small stage-upon-the-stage served to thrust his carefully com-posed figure compositions forward, in a manner that virtually eliminated any sense of a "fourth wall" separating actor and spectator. Thoor's com-ment is particularly apt in this connection: "This is theatre that interests itself almost exclusively in human beings and hardly at all in the things that surround them."

The "full reality" that, Strindberg insists, underlies the anguished pil-grimage of his protagonist is an inner reality – a magic realism of the soul that Bergman's interpretation delineated with laser-sharp clarity and also with a strong undertone of black humour and irony. "Strictly speaking only one character in the play is real," commented the critic for *GT* (Göteborg). "Whatever else happens on the stage may appear more or less real, but in the last analysis it is all a projection of the fantasies, mem-ories, dreams, and imagination of the Unknown." The painful journey of this figure was amplified, in this director's production, into "a thrilling voyage of discovery into a spiritual landscape . . . where no values are constant, and where reality changes shape with all the remorseless, un-predictable logic of a nightmare. Figures, thoughts, situations recur, lines of dialogue rebound among the characters like symphonic leitmotifs. It is a drama that embraces wisdom and madness, werewolves and beggars, hell and heaven."[28] Bergman was relatively uninterested in a conven-tionally religious approach to *To Damascus*, as a drama of conversion and atonement. Instead, he was far more concerned with the emotional, lyrical, and even social aspects of the central character's spiritual jour-ney. "He demystifies the drama," wrote Bengt Jahnsson in *Dagens Nyheter* (February 2). "At times the projection screen in the background is filled by a searching eye. But this is not God's eye watching the Unknown and us. The memory of the past watches over his actions, intensifying his horror and anxiety. Our victims watch over us."

Jan-Olof Strandberg's virtuoso performance as the Unknown thus carved out an intensely human and existentially divided protagonist, vacillating in an instant from tenderness to savage sarcasm, hopelessly trapped between rebellious arrogance and a gnawing self-torment. "Not infrequently he is so naïve and comical that we laugh at him," *Expressen* observed. "But then suddenly the poetry in his words blossoms forth, the magic is there, and it falls silent around him." Transformation was the governing theatrical technique in this production, and this in turn established a tragicomic irony as its predominant mode. The visual high point of the transformation trope was the stunning transmogrification of the Goldmaker's Banquet, where with the swiftness and illogic of a dream the Unknown found himself cast, without a transition, from the happy illusion of the banquet into the inferno of disgrace and degradation. This scene emerged as the culmination of a perpetual ironic process, in which every potential happiness in the Unknown's existence – love, family ties, children, success even royalty statements – has been suddenly transformed into dust and ashes in his hands. For Chaplin or Beckett, such a process is comedic, evoking what the latter calls the mirthless laugh, the *risus purus* ("in a word the laugh that laughs at that which is unhappy"). Swedish audiences and critics accustomed to the grave Strindberg of the Molander tradition were evidently a little taken aback by the Beckettian dimension of Strandberg's performance. "He presents a role instead of playing a character," Leif Zern declared in an American interview. "He is an actor with a great sensitivity for the theatrical and comical, with a feeling for space, a physical actor." Astonishingly, however, this critic cites these features as negative qualities in a Strindberg actor. "As a result, his [Unknown] became a rather comic figure; it gave the production a rather ironic tone . . . One night almost think Bergman didn't take the play seriously, or at any rate did not take the character of the [Unknown] really seriously."[29] It needs hardly be added that Bergman would have taken both play and character fully as seriously as Beckett takes "comedy."

Bergman staged the initial, hypnotic encounter between the Unknown and the Lady in a manner that differed sharply from the older convention of locating it in a more or less "real" environment. The scene was played against a projected background that evoked a dreamlike, spider-web image of a Gothic church portal and a house façade. The only furnishing on the stage was a simple wooden bench, around which the rhythm of the moves of approach and withdrawal, union and separation, was choreographed with all the precision of a pas de deux.

6 A radically simplified setting for the initial meeting of the Unknown (Jan-Olof
Strandberg) and the Lady (Helena Brodin) on the street corner was created by Marik
Vos for the Bergman production of *To Damascus I–II* at Dramaten in 1974. Here, the
sole suggestion of "place" on the unlocalized stage is provided by the spidery projection
of a Gothic church in the background.

Helena Brodin, dressed in cool green as the Lady, created an intense
but restrained impression in this scene as a listener holding back her
passion, "a well-dressed woman of the world who watches this strange
and singular man with interest. Later, love and hatred obliterate the
restrained façade, and the strife between the man and the pregnant
woman takes on the frenzy that we usually call Strindbergian," wrote
Carl Hammarén in *Nerikes Allehanda* (Örebro). As their first meeting
drew to a close with the Lady's impulsive kiss and passionate decla-
ration ("Come, my liberator!"), an inquisitive human eye gazed down
ironically from the projection screen. The reason was a very practical
one: "It is essential to finish on the Unknown," the director noted, for
in this version the central character remained throughout the play the

controlling consciousness through which all its events are perceived and recorded.

The first station on the couple's journey was the home of the Physician, the savage husband from whom the Unknown has rashly vowed to free the fairy princess. Three low screens and a corresponding trio of simple chairs, arranged to enclose and confine the action, made up the "veranda" setting for this scene. A naïve triptych depicting Swedish country scenes adorned the rear screen, as the merest hint of the elaborate milieu that Strindberg described and Grabow tried to paint. Here in this haunted house of ticking death clocks, Ulf Johansson's vengeful doctor ("bizarre at first, later terrifying in his threats and hatred") confronted the Unknown with the most sinister of his exhibits – Caesar, the laurel-crowned madman who dwells in the cellar and in whom the Unknown is horrified to recognize a grotesque mirror image of himself. "Why does it all come back again – corpses and beggars and human destinies and childhood memories," he cried as he fell to his knees in desperate supplication in this production.

Unlike the localities of these first two incidents, which were not revisited in Bergman's version, the "kitchen" of the Lady's childhood home became a recurrent station on the Unknown's journey, reserved in particular for his humiliating confrontations with the taunting and remorseless mother of his companion. Bergman returned to this setting four times in all, for it was also here that, in Part II, the vindictive Mother robbed her son-in-law of all joy in his newborn daughter. Each time the kitchen reappeared, the sparse furnishings of the scene were slightly rearranged; the only element that remained constant was a plain white screen upon which, as its sole adornment, a large crucifix was prominently displayed. (When turned around the screen had a rose-coloured reverse side for use in the three Rose Chamber scenes in this version.) There was thus no attempt to provide a picture of a recognizable place – that is, Strindberg's "roomy kitchen with white calcimine walls" in all its details. Instead, the spectator was faced with a recurrent and distinctly disturbing image of a state of mind, the harsh, hell-fire religious orthodoxy signified by the iconic crucifix. A photograph of the scene shows the Mother and the Maid joined with the old Grandfather in prayer in the opening moments of the fifth scene in Bergman's version (Strindberg's 2.v). What this picture omits to show is the director's theatricalized use of total stage space. Although "offstage" while their predicament is being so unfeelingly discussed by the others, the Unknown and the Lady were, in fact, already standing in full view to the right of the platform, waiting

7 For the Kitchen in the Lady's childhood home, one of the most oppressive and recurrent stations on the Unknown's journey, the Bergman production used only a small, bare screen, a prominently displayed crucifix, and a few pieces of heavy furniture.

silently to make their "entrance" and place themselves at the mercy of the family's grudging charity.

Often, the most effective of the "close-up" moments in this production made use of no scenery at all. Such an instance was the moving scene in which the Unknown is reunited with the Lady by the sea, with which Bergman concluded Part I in his adaptation. Both the platform and the stage space surrounding it were completely bare and empty. The overall visual impression was, at the outset, one of winter whiteness and extreme cold. The only scenographic accent was provided by projections of shining cloud formations on the black background, gradually dissolving in the closing moments of the scene to a haunting, impressionistic image of shipmast crosses looming up on the horizon. A short excerpt from Bergman's promptbook illustrates both the concision of his text and the nature of his emotional orchestration of it:

THE UNKNOWN Put your hand in mine, and let us leave this place forever. (*He reaches out his hand. She takes it. He lowers his head, she kisses him on the mouth, and he rests his head against her shoulder.*) Are you tired?

THE LADY Not any longer! (*Music*)

THE UNKNOWN (*Facing the sea*) It's growing dark and the clouds are gathering . . .

THE LADY (*Quickly consoling him*) Don't look at the clouds . . .

THE UNKNOWN And over there? What is that?

THE LADY (*Consoling*) Only a sunken ship!

THE UNKNOWN (*In a whisper*) Three crosses! – What new Golgotha awaits us now?

THE LADY (*Consoling*) But they're white: that's a good sign!

THE UNKNOWN (*Looking at her*) Can anything good happen to us ever again?

THE LADY (*Consoling smile*) Yes, but not right away.

THE UNKNOWN (*Laying his arm on her shoulder*) Let us go!

Bergman's *Damascus* established a dynamic rhythm of contrasts between these intimate close-up scenes and another kind of stage composition entirely. In these *changements à vue* (Bergman's own term), nightmare penetrated reality in an instant, and the Unknown suddenly found his private demons and innermost fears transmogrified into hideous scenes of public condemnation and disgrace. At these moments the background opened, the small platform stage was absorbed into the new figure composition, and the Unknown became the focus of a mass spectacle that was always different and yet always the same. Each new public mortification became an amplification of the previous one. And, in one form or another, the Unknown's constant companion in these ordeals was the shadowy dual character of the Beggar–Confessor created by Anders Ek. "Visible or invisible, he is always present, prodding or provoking the Unknown," Hammarén observed in *Nerikes Allehanda*. "Ek holds the stage with a combination of the clown's jesting – the trait that seems to run through to the very core of his personality – and a massive, almost annihilating authority." It was he who guided the Unknown on his journey, and he who commented on every station along the way. In the guise of the Latin-quoting Beggar – the protagonist's double, with the mark of Cain upon his forehead – he brought down public ridicule on the Unknown in the opening scene on the crowded street corner, when the brown-clad Pallbearers suddenly materialized and just as suddenly disappeared again. His attack became fiercer and more harrowing as the Dominican confessor in the Asylum scene, where the Unknown sat cramped in his chair like a condemned prisoner while the litany of curses from Deuteronomy rained down over him. At a long table in the background sat the grotesque, soup-eating participants in the ghostly supper – Caesar, the Beggar, the Physician, the grieving parents, the cruelly treated sister, the abandoned wife and her two children, and, farthest to the right, the Lady, who sits knitting rather than eating. "Decide whether they are the same [i.e., identical to the actual characters from the Unknown's past]! No, they should wear masks and [different] costumes," reads a note in the director's script.

The central scene in this theatrical paraphrase of *To Damascus* was not, however, the Unknown's ordeal in the asylum, but rather his abject humiliation at the satirical Goldmaker's Banquet, which occurs towards the end of Part II. Bergman condensed the earlier scene in the laboratory into a brief, somnambulistic dream sequence that emphasized the destructive fanaticism underlying the Unknown's desire to make gold:

> ...so as to destroy the world order, to bring chaos, you see! (*More heavily*) I am the destroyer, the annihilator, the arsonist of the universe, and when everything lies in ashes (*more heavily*), I shall run *hungering* through the ruins and rejoice in this thought: (*more heavily*) that *I have done* this, I who have witnessed the final page of the world's history – which can now be regarded as finished.

Absorbed in his anarchistic vision, the Unknown readily allows himself to be acclaimed and decorated at what he conceives as a glittering testimonial banquet held in his honour. In this production it consisted of a smirking, bug-eyed troll court of absurdly uniformed gentlemen and enormous, bare-breasted society matrons. No sooner had the unsuspecting protagonist been crowned with laurel and hailed by the tawdry multitude as the Great Goldmaker than this bizarre assembly began to undergo a metamorphosis. Swiftly, in accordance with a carefully choreographed four-step pattern of visible transformation, the beribboned officers and gentlemen were turned into beggars, vagabonds, and *clochards*, while the fine ladies became whores and sluts. By the time Caesar, the Physician's madman, had launched his irrational, virtually Hitlerian tirade against the Unknown, the change was complete. What the latter had perceived as a "royal celebration" and a "sincere tribute" that had restored "[his] faith in himself" was now an ugly, shabby, and distinctly hostile collection of ruffians gathered in a dingy café.

Virtually every reviewer had words of praise for the startling visual effect of this scene. One or two were even prepared to congratulate the director on having made, for once, an acceptably anticapitalistic comment on the hollowness of the ruling classes. "As far as one can remember, this is the first time that Ingmar Bergman has uttered a word in the sociopolitical debate; the scene is a comment on the representative establishment and its relationship to those it represents," ventured Åke Perlström in *Göteborgs-Posten* (February 2). However, such generalizations are of little help in clarifying the thematic relevance of this episode to Bergman's overall interpretation of *To Damascus* and, indeed, to his conception of Strindberg's drama as a whole. One might well argue that, above all, the Goldmaker's Banquet became in this production the ultimate nightmare of humiliation, a dream-within-the-dream that is watched with horror by the sleepwalking protagonist. Its ruling irony lay in the sense that the ridicule and scorn heaped upon the dreamer are always made worse by his own gnawing suspicion that they may after all be justified and represent the truth about himself.

A projection of disintegrating house façades in the background provided a concise visual image of the aftermath of the grotesque banquet. In this final "public" scene, the Unknown returned to the dingy café in the hope that "a mud bath" might "harden [his] skin against the stings of life." Instead, in a macabre atmosphere filled with writhing, grasping beggars, cripples, and prostitutes, his spirit was poisoned and his life virtually sucked out of him by the savage hypnotic power of the "werewolf" Physician. The ceremonial entrance of the hooded Confessor, carrying the monstrance to "a dying man inside," coincided with the Unknown's horrified realization that he, too, was perhaps dead without ever knowing it. "The dead claim that no one knows the difference," the Physician agreed "with ghastly emphasis."

8 Near the end of Part II in the Bergman production of *To Damascus*, in a dingy café filled with grotesque and sinister figures, the Unknown is figuratively destroyed by the psychic power of the savage Physician (Ulf Johansson, right).

After the Unknown's "death" in this scene, the final stages on his journey passed swiftly, and they led toward a distinctly ambivalent resolution of his plight. Bergman's abridgement omitted several intermediate, expository steps in the process, including the Unknown's anguished dream-encounter with his abandoned children, the destruction of Caesar and the Physician, and the consultation between the Lady and the Confessor about his salvation. Instead, the closing moments in this version were tightly concentrated on the last of the "scenes from a marriage." Our final glimpse into the connubial Rose Chamber revealed a deadlock from which there could be no escape – a timeless, airless domestic hell from which the Unknown was powerless to extricate himself. ("The Unknown is locked into his position. He cannot move an inch. He is in catatonic paralysis," reads one of the director's notes.) In this context, the Confessor's option of a monastic existence represented at least a kind of exit visa – a very open and ambiguous alternative to the ironies and torments of this life's inferno. The end result became, in the opinion of many observers, a drama of atonement in which the central character never repents. As he went down on his knees to the Lady before leaving her to follow his "terrible friend," Strandberg's actions as the Unknown provided no firm assurance that his ferocious struggle with the riddle of existence had been resolved. Rather, the performance condensed the final moments of Strindberg's somewhat discursive conclusion into an emotionally charged tableau that served to underscore the openness of the ending:

(She goes forward to him, falls to her knees, embraces him and kisses him lingeringly on the mouth. Then she rises. Still kneeling, he lifts a hand to his mouth. Then he rises and goes toward the priest. He reaches out his hand:)
Come, priest, before I change my mind!

More than one critic called the ending "only the beginning of a new round." And yet the experience of the struggle itself – the sense of having gone through a trial that may turn out to be a blessing in disguise – inevitably suggests its own kind of purification and reconciliation in Strindberg's scheme of things.

TO DAMASCUS IN THE CONTEMPORARY THEATRE

As Bergman's radically simplified, actor-oriented approach demonstrated, *To Damascus* has long since ceased to be a technical challenge to the resources of modern stagecraft. Instead, its effect on a contemporary audience depends not on the ingenuity of a succession of stage settings, but on the intense inner reality of its emotional encounters. The topography of the play is the purely imaginary topography of a dream – or an empty stage. The discordant rhythm of clashing moods and emotions is the true reality of the Unknown's journey. But the logic of the play is not psychological, rooted in discernible causes and explicable motivations. At this point in his career, as we have seen, Strindberg had turned away from a theatre of character to what Jean-Paul Sartre later calls a theatre of situation, shaped not by a preoccupation with "character" as the sum total of psychological traits, but rather by a concern with the dramatic situation that ultimately defines the characters in a play, with the choices it affords (or denies) them, and with the limits within which they are confined on all sides. In the new, arcanic style of play he inaugurated with *To Damascus*, Strindberg no longer had any use for the naturalistic model of drama, with its basis in causality, logical sequence, and psychologically motivated character.

Unfortunately for Strindberg's later plays (and for the whole avant-garde tradition for which they supplied a blueprint), the "existentialist" rejection of characterological theatre seems no more congenial to North American directors and actors today than when Sartre first proclaimed it, in the pages of *Theatre Arts* in 1946.[30] A recent case in point would be the first professional Canadian production of *To Damascus*, which the Equity Showcase Theatre presented in Toronto in 1994. The Stranger (as English-language translations frequently insist on calling *Den Okände*) skipped across the stage, struck slapstick declamatory poses, and even dropped his pants in an effort to overcome the play's perceived deficiencies with his parody. "Given [the play's] overstated and undermotivated characters, dreary concerns, preposterous plotting, and artificial-sounding language . . . [director Adam] Nashman has wisely elected to play for the laughs wherever possible and otherwise concentrate on clever staging, deftly executed movement, and pretty pictures," declared the critic for *The Globe and Mail* (December 3, 1994). The clever staging and pretty pictures to which this reviewer alludes were of the unspecific, all-purpose variety, achieved by complex rearrangements of an enormous white curtain that was at times suspended from a selection of hooks, at other points folded on the floor or rippled to suggest a seascape.

A more representative example of the continued evolution of a contemporary performance style for *To Damascus* was furnished by the impressive German revival of Part I staged by Erwin Axer at the Residenztheater in Munich in 1983. Axer's capable ensemble included Martin

Benrath as the Unknown and Christine Ostermayer as the Lady; even the veteran Kurt Meisel, who had played the Unknown in a three-hour adaptation of the entire trilogy at the Munich Kammerspiele in 1956, appeared as the Old Man. Both in the simplicity of its scenography and in its correspondingly strong emphasis on the movements, groupings, and facial expressions of the actors, the Axer performance could well be seen as a further extension of Bergman's non-representational method. (The latter was himself one of the principal directors at the Residenz at this time but had no connection with Axer's work on the play.) The scene photos reproduced here reveal the tendency toward an even more pronounced isolation of the human figures in a pool of light which, like Bergman's platform, functioned as a focusing device. Moreover, these images also help to situate this contemporary production within a broader scenographic tradition that extends back to the premiere of the play in 1900.

Axer's scenography again called attention to the stage as a stage – in this instance a steeply raked platform of broad rustic planks. The meeting of the Unknown and the Lady in the opening scene took place not on a realistic street corner (as in Molander) or even before a stylized church projection (as in Bergman), but rather in a dreamscape; seated on a simple wooden park bench, Benrath and Ostermayer seemed to occupy a small island of light in a sea of encroaching darkness. Later in the same scene, as the six brown-clad Pallbearers appeared out of the dark and the Proprietor came forward to take orders, the addition of a small, round table was sufficient to convey the impression of an outdoor café.

The atmosphere of ominous, even oppressive gloom in Axer's performance grew steadily stronger as the journey unfolded. The photograph of the first Kitchen scene clearly recalls Bergman's arrangement of this moment, but the heavy door in the background, the empty black cross on the wall behind the Old Man, and the shaft of light coming through the narrow, window-like aperture on his left all contribute to a much darker impression of a dungeon or even a tomb. This visual metaphor of imprisonment, which recurred in different forms throughout this production, is especially evident in Axer's stark image of the Asylum scene. Here, hemmed in by the two heavy refectory tables in the photo, the Unknown appears trapped in a nightmarish inferno of light that washes out and obscures the faces of his accusers. In the background, the view of black space intensifies the sense of his utter isolation. Listening to the parasensical torrent of cures being read over him, Benrath's gowned figure seems both pilgrim and prisoner, at once the acolyte and the sacrificial victim in some strange rite.

9 The fanatical Mother (Annemarie Wernicke) and the Old Man (Kurt Meisel) in the first Kitchen scene in Erwin Axer's production of *To Damascus* (Munich Residenztheater, 1983). Ewa Starowleyska's stark, unlocalized scenography invites comparison with the Bergman production, but conveys an even darker and more claustrophobic impression.

9 In Axer's staging of the Asylum scene, the gowned figure of the Unknown (Martin Benrath) appears as both pilgrim and prisoner as he endures the curses read over him by the Confessor (Karl-Heinz Pelser).

Particularly in its succession of powerful visual images, this German revival of *To Damascus I* was far darker in tone and heavier in texture than earlier Swedish productions have generally been. Some would indeed quarrel with this approach, agreeing with Evert Sprinchorn that such an interpretation neglects "that strange Strindbergian mixture of humor and melancholy, of tragic anguish and comic frustration. And if it is not there when the play is staged, something very essential to the spirit of the whole will be lacking."[31] In the last analysis, however, no single approach or performance choice will ever succeed in encompassing the full range of this play's complex tonal variations. As one of the truly seminal works of modernist art, it foreshadows Joyce's *Ulysses* on the one hand and the artistic principles of Picasso and Braque on the other. More to the point for our purposes, it also implemented a new theatrical style on which both *A Dream Play* and *The Ghost Sonata* would continue to draw and depend. These two other masterpieces of Strindberg's post-Inferno period are by now more frequently read and performed than *To Damascus*, but neither of them possesses the dramaturgical clarity or the absorbing subjective perspective of Strindberg's first dream play.

3

A theatre of dreams: *A Dream Play*

"Understand *The Dream Play?*" Strindberg asks in a letter to his tireless German translator Emil Schering (May 13, 1902), shortly after sending him a copy of his newest work, *Ett drömspel*:

Everything absurd becomes probable. People flit past and a few traits are sketched in, the sketches merge, a single character dissolves into several, who merge into one again. Time and space do not exist; a minute is like many years; no seasons; the snow covers the countryside in summer, the lime tree turns yellow, and then green again . . .

This passage is, of course, a close paraphrase of the Author's Foreword with which Strindberg introduced the published text of his play. This very familiar prefatory note has sometimes been misinterpreted as evidence that *A Dream Play* is essentially formless, extemporaneous, and even incoherent. Conscious perhaps of this misapprehension, Strindberg added some key paragraphs to his explanatory note when the play at last reached the stage in 1907. This amended version of the Foreword, which was placed in the director's script but not published at the time, emphasizes the controlled musical construction of the work and the "strict musical treatment" to which its voices have been subjected:

As far as the loose, disconnected shape of the play is concerned, this too is only apparent. On closer examination, the composition is seen to be quite firm and solid – a symphony, polyphonic, now and then like a figure with a constantly recurring main theme, which is repeated in all registers and varied by the more than thirty voices.[1]

In the same letter to Schering, Strindberg describes the dominant theme to which he alludes here: "Indra's daughter has come down to earth in order to find out how mankind lives, and thus discovers how hard life is. And the hardest thing of all is hurting others, which one is forced to do if one wants to live." The variations on this simple fairy-tale theme are complex and intricately counterpointed in a pattern of cascading visual and verbal recurrences, correspondences, and contradictions. Exactly like a musical composition or a non-representational painting, *A Dream Play* is thus not "about" something: its form is the direct expression of its inner reality, its emotional meaning for an audience. In this way the play depends for its effect entirely on the same power of emotional suggestion as music or abstract art.

Strindberg was, moreover, fully aware that he was in the process of devising a new kind of drama – one that is at odds with both the Aristotelian drama of strict causality (*Oedipus Rex* or *Ghosts*, for example) and the drama of character (*Hamlet* or *Hedda Gabler*). "*The Dream Play*," he wrote to Schering, "is a new form, which is my invention." Unfortunately, he had no success in persuading those involved in the first production of the play to listen to his ideas. To his chagrin, the play had its world premiere (April 17, 1907) not at Dramaten but at Svenska teatern (The Swedish Theatre), where the precedent set by Grandinson's effective staging of *To Damascus* was disregarded. Also ignored were Strindberg's explicitly anti-realistic stage directions, which call for "stylized murals suggesting at the same time space, architecture, and landscape" to remain at the sides throughout, supplemented only by changing backdrops. The playwright implored his director, Victor Castegren, to try to "transform the drama into visual representation without materializing it too much" (*LIT*, 293). Castegren dutifully procured a sciopticon projector from a theatre in Dresden, where it had been used for a production of *Faust* (a work for which earlier models of the so-called *laterna magica* were known to have been used in Germany as far back as 1819). After some unsuccessful experiments with back projections, however, this possibility was soon abandoned. Albert Ranft, the business-minded theatre owner, also rejected the *Damascus* alternative of arches and backcloths, of which Strindberg had obviously been thinking when he wrote *A Dream Play*. In the end, as the playwright put it, "the only thing left to do was to 'go to Grabow'"(*LIT*, 294).

Without the advantage of Grandinson's ingenuity, Carl Grabow's colourful but conventionally pictorial designs resulted in a heavily realistic scenography that was, in Strindberg's view, "too material for the dream." Awkward changes of scene and inept lighting techniques disrupted the play's mesmeric flow of fleeting, shifting images. What symbolism there was in the endeavour seems to have been heavy-handed; the forestage was "transformed into a field of poppies, the symbol of sleep, while the stage behind it was framed by an arch, painted with garlands

10 The Growing Castle, its gilded roof rising about a forest of giant hollyhocks, in a design by Carl Grabow for the world premiere of *A Dream Play* (Svenska teatern, Stockholm, 1907).

of poppies, within which the dream scenes appeared and disappeared."[2] Generally rather baffled, the reviewers of this first production were inclined to address the play as a reading drama that defied adequate stage representation. "The task is so incredibly difficult that one hardly even has a right to make comments," Tor Hedberg remarked in *Svenska Dagbladet* (April 18, 1907). This critic was troubled in particular by the production's inability to accomplish "the transformations of the scenes, one into another – the visualization of the idea associations which, for the reader, are what make the strongest impression." In other words, Grabow's painted drops simply followed one after another, with no effort made to suggest the system of correspondences inherent in those key scenic elements that change and yet remain the same – the omnipresent cloverleaf door, the linden tree that becomes a coat-rack and then a candelabra, and so on.

The thorny problem of an appropriate acting style for Strindberg's dream plays again became a major issue here. "I have heard it said that the settings ought to be more stylized, in order to convey some impression of unreality, of dream," wrote Daniel Fallström in *Nya Dagligt Allehanda* (April 18). "But if so, the actors in this stylized environment would also have to become stylized. And a stylized actor – brrr!" The type of acting adopted by Castegren's ensemble appears to have wavered unsteadily between the conversational tone of naturalism and the intoned symbolist declamation advocated by Lugné-Poë and his school. Only Harriet Bosse, now divorced from Strindberg but still in contact with him, seems to have captured the spirit of the play fully. As Indra's Daughter, wrote Bo Bergman, "her pure diction shone as always, and her soft, almost floating tread had just the right ethereal quality for the daughter of a divinity" (*Dagens Nyheter*).

Strindberg's own ideas about acting had undergone radical change, and Bosse's understated, allusive style was obviously his new ideal. Particularly after he and August Falck founded Intima teatern in the autumn of 1907, he was more inclined to put his ideas on the subject into writing, in the form of memorandums of advice to the Intima ensemble that he ultimately published in 1908 as *Open Letters to the Intimate Theatre*. As a poet of the theatre Strindberg, like Yeats, regarded the beauty of language as the centre of the theatrical experience, to which other elements of the production should be subordinated. Like his great Irish contemporary, he exhorted his actors to resist restless gestures and movements that would only detract from the impact of the spoken word. The actor in Strindberg's theatre was to keep the audience in mind at all times, speaking clearly and slowly so that the words become a string of pearls, rather than adopting a staccato delivery that emulated "a wretched conversational tone of voice." "Take it broadly, like a singer, enjoy hearing your own voice, and even if you increase the pace, maintain this *legato*," he wrote to Anna Flygare, one of his most accomplished actors, in a personal letter (February 3, 1908). Playing in this way, he continues, "each word doesn't require facial expressions and gestures, for that is old-fashioned." In his emphasis on the pre-eminent importance of the actor's control, he sounds at times almost like Brecht: "The actor must control his role and not let the role control him: i.e., not let himself be so intoxicated or enchanted by the words that he loses his head . . . The actor should be so strong that he remains unmoved by his fellow actors and does not let them tempt him into their strains" (*LIT*, 36). He is careful to qualify his ideas, however, in a manner that sets them apart from Brecht's concept of Verfremdung: "But the danger here is being too conscious [of the role], so that one succumbs to cold calculation, speculation of effects, emphasis, signalling, display, etc."

In essence, Strindberg's goal was a restoration of the modern actor's dissipated power of poetic and spiritual expressiveness. His ideas on the subject derived from many sources. One particular passage that seems to have stirred his imagination is underlined in his personal copy of Georg Fuchs' *Die Schaubühne der Zukunft* (1905):

The Japanese actor does not shout, does not make noise; voices are hardly ever raised on the stage, hardly anything happens that goes beyond the polite tone of refined society. And yet the Japanese actor achieves dramatic effects of an intensity that we have never known.[3]

As we know, the stylized expressiveness of oriental theatre appealed strongly to Fuchs, Yeats, Craig, and other modernists as an alternative to the naturalism they deplored – and Strindberg eagerly joined them in their struggle to displace the naturalistic mode of theatre he himself had helped to introduce in the 1880s. It is easy to see why he was drawn to Fuchs, for whom the purpose of all such stylization was to subject the decorative and pictorial elements of the theatre to the "inner" voice of the play, by facilitating the plastic and spatial movements of the human body upon which dramatic art ultimately depends. The spoken text alone is, in his view, never enough to reveal the inner emotional texture of the play. Rather, the director must enable the actor's movements, gestures, and mime to probe and reveal an area beyond the spoken word, and to do so the closest possible rapport must be established with the spectator, whose direct emotional participation in the inner action of the drama is essential. This "intensification of our existence," which Fuchs finds to be the theatre's chief task, is precisely what Strindberg sought to achieve in *A Dream Play* – and it was precisely what he found lacking in Castegren's unsatisfactory performance of it.

During the years following the miscarried premiere of *A Dream Play*, he continued to grapple with a wide variety of schemes and plans for a simplified, stylized, even emblematic restaging of it on the impossibly small stage at Intima teatern. He had now reached the conclusion that only a radically dematerialized, non-representational style of staging was appropriate, even for his history plays. A distinct change in popular taste had already taken place in this regard, he was convinced: "By the end of the century . . . the imaginative became active, the material gave way to the immaterial, the spoken word became the major thing on the stage" (*LIT*, 289–90). Four months after the opening of Intima teatern, Falck's effectively stylized revival of *Queen Christina* [*Kristina*] was performed on an unadorned stage using only a reddish-brown velvet backdrop and side wings covered in the same material. In the wake of this very successful drapery-stage experiment the playwright took to the proselytizing of this kind of staging as a universal solution for all plays. Above all, it confirmed his faith in the liberating power of the non-representational approach. "Simplicity provides the solemn calm and silence which alone makes it possible for the artist to hear his role," he wrote to his partner a few weeks after this production (May 9, 1908). "By keeping the scenery simple, what matters emerges: the character, role, speech, expression, gestures."

Although a similar drapery-stage approach to *A Dream Play* was considered as one possibility, Strindberg continually bombarded Falck (who resisted the whole idea of performing this complex work in a chamber-theatre format) with alternative suggestions. These staging proposals for *A Dream Play*, which Falck transcribes in his published memoir of his five-year association with Strindberg, ranged from drapes or projected scenery to symbolically painted side wings or even rotating triangular flats in the manner of Greek *periaktoi*. His account also includes a rough sketch made by Strindberg, showing a permanent unit set made up of three pairs of side panels painted to suggest elements from the various scenes in the play (hollyhocks, the cloverleaf door, an iron stove, an organ, ship masts, and so on). The background depicts the dome of a castle rising above the clouds. "The ceiling [borders] clouds, and the upper part of the wings also clouds," reads a note scribbled on the sketch.[4]

None of these speculative ideas for staging *A Dream Play* was ever realized in practice during Strindberg's lifetime. Soon after his death, however, the play became – and to a certain extent still is – a lodestone for avant-garde experiments and scenographic images of all sorts. Particularly its early German productions tended to transport it into a realm of expressionist fantasy which, while a world apart from the conventionality and literalism of its world premiere, was still no less cumbersome, no less insensitive to Strindberg's plea for simplicity and his attendant dismay at productions that create "a 'materialization phenomenon' instead of the intended dematerialization" (*LIT*, 294).

DREAMS FANTASTICAL, WORLDS APART

The two productions of *A Dream Play* staged by Max Reinhardt, one in Swedish and the other in German, in 1921 are generally considered the most significant – or even the only significant – performances of the play prior to Olof Molander's definitive revival of it in 1935. In fact, however, Reinhardt's work was preceded and followed by several other notable attempts to translate the complex dynamics of Strindberg's dream-play dramaturgy into viable performance practice. The German premiere

of the play, directed by Rudolf Bernauer at his influential Theater im
der Königgrätzerstrasse in 1916, was probably the most popular and
most problematic of these attempts. "Playful" and "whimsical" were
recurrent adjectives in the reviews of a performance that, according to
Emil Faktor in *Berliner Börsen-Courier* (March 18, 1916), "filled the spectator
with irresistible fairy-tale pleasure . . . It was an evening of sights and
delights." The amelioristic tone of Bernauer's interpretation is clearly
evident in Faktor's passing comment that "there is a great deal of humour
in that mock-serious proclamation: 'Human beings are to be pitied.'"
Overwhelmed by the horrors of the war and threatened by a critical food
shortage brought on by the Allied blockade of Germany, the residents
of the capital literally flocked to Bernauer's *Traumspiel* as a hopeful fairy
tale of redemption from the "dream" of earthly grief and pain. The
refutation of this escapist view was definitely on Reinhardt's mind when
he in turn mounted his own deeply pessimistic and disturbing version of
A Dream Play five years later.

The effect of the Bernauer production hinged to a large extent on the
ingenious scenography of Svend Gade, who in this instance was more
successful than in the production of *To Damascus* he had designed for
Victor Barnowsky two years earlier. Without using a revolving stage,
Gade expedited the flow of his scene changes in *A Dream Play* by introducing a starry blue transparency that covered the entire proscenium
opening and remained in place throughout the performance. An opaque
front curtain when the stage behind it was in darkness, it became a misty,
dream-like filter when the action was illuminated. (Lest one suppose that
this was some unprecedented finesse of the New Stagecraft, it bears not-
ing that Samuel Phelps had achieved much the same effect with a green
scrim he used for *A Midsummer-Night's Dream* – in 1853. "And not only do
the scenes melt dream-like one into another, but over all the fairy portion
of the play there is a haze thrown by a curtain of green gauze placed
between the actors and the audience," the incomparable Henry Morley
wrote at the time: " . . . its influence is everywhere felt; it subdues the flesh
and blood of the actors into something more nearly resembling dream-
figures, and incorporates more completely the actors with the scenes,
throwing the same green fairy tinge and the same mist over all."[5]) To
make his point twice – "doppelt hält besser," as Siegfried Jacobsohn puts
it – Gade also enclosed the theatre's proscenium in an immense elliptical
frame, "so that one does not forget that this is a dream play."[6] Later his-
torians have offered suggestions that this giant oval-shaped frame might
be meant to signify an eye or perhaps even the Ear of the god Indra

who, as the Daughter tells the Poet in the first Fingal's Cave scene, "listens to mankind's complaints." Surely, however, the salient point is that the fourth wall created by this arch and the blue gauze curtain that covered it established a sense of the stage as peep-show – a magical box into which Bernauer's audience (not unlike an audience of the mid-nineteenth century) peered, as detached spectators, at the "pleasing" theatrical fantasy unfolding before them.

When it comes to Strindberg's later plays, however, a clear distinction must be drawn between "fantasy" and "dream." In his world, the reality of the latter ("the torment of the dream," as he puts it in his Foreword) is always inescapable. Hence, if *A Dream Play* is presented simply as harmless fantasy, its dangerous modernist perceptions about the collapse of language, meaning, and the differentiation between dream and so-called objective reality are subverted. As this happens, the play itself is transported back, as it were, to the realm of its popular forebears – the Viennese *Zauberpossen* of Raimund, the *eventyrkomedier* of Hans Christian Andersen, and *Lucky Per's Journey*, in which Strindberg draws freely on both the aforementioned models. In the Bernauer-Gade collaboration, the metaphysical framework of the play – which, as we know, was added by Strindberg as an afterthought – became the guarantee of a fairy-tale solution. The gold-clad Daughter of Indra (Irene Triesch) descended to earth in an elaborate golden aureole (a "mandorla," Gade called it, meaning an almond-shaped glory machine of the kind used for the transport of divinities in early paintings and Renaissance theatre) and she returned to heaven by the same route, while surrealistic tongues of fire shot from the Growing Castle and a stylized chrysanthemum sprouted from its roof. Triesch played the Daughter entirely as an observer, with an inquisitive eye and a quiet, watchful attitude. Faktor's review in *Berliner Börsen-Courier* described her as "a tormented human being when she forgot herself for a moment, an intense emotional interpreter when she remembered her divine origins." After Reinhardt's Berlin production in 1921, Norbert Falk observed in retrospect: "Triesch's acute spirituality gave her a superiority that made her earthly suffering seem willed, like an episode allowed to take place" – in contrast to Helene Thimig, Reinhardt's Agnes, who "forgets that she is both Indra's Daughter and a spectator."[7] In this way, Triesch's conscious aloofness in the Bernauer performance accentuated the dominant tone of fairy tale and make-believe – the sense of "an episode allowed to take place," watched with interest by this stage spectator and her counterparts in the auditorium.

Both lighting and music contributed significantly to the oneiric atmosphere established by Bernauer's mise-en-scène. Surrounded in black velvet, the stage space was illuminated in a silvery grey light that blurred contours and conveyed the impression of a bleached dream landscape. Viewed in this strange light, groups of figures appeared to be shrouded in mist, like shadowy apparitions, while the Officer (Ludwig Hartau), the Lawyer (Friedrich Kayssler), and the Poet (Alfred Abel) seemed literally to merge, one into another, so as to become a single personality. The dominant force in this triad was unquestionably Hartau's Officer, with "something fleeting, something ethereal about both his voice and his figure, as if only a part of his life was being revealed by him" (*Berliner Tageblatt*). In his tribute to Hartau's performance, Jacobsohn saw what most other critics did not – the dark side of Strindberg's vision: "How this man transformed himself, how he became a phantom of himself, the way in which his laughter acquired a dying fall – this is acting of the highest calibre, and it brings something bizarre to this most bitter dream play."[8]

The "disjunctive but ostensibly logical form of a dream" that Strindberg's play seeks to replicate was communicated in a very direct, sensory way by the musical score composed for this production by Emil von Reznicek. Written for a compact ensemble made up of winds, muted trumpet, and cello, Reznicek's score was dissonant and even cacophonic at times, but its emulation of Wagner's leitmotif technique also provided for melodic moments, such as the melancholy cello passage that continually sang the play's principal refrain: "Human beings are to be pitied." The atonal harmonies of the score reconstituted some of Strindberg's own musical suggestions, replacing the Bach Toccata with which Ugly Edith demolishes the ballroom waltz at Fairhaven with new music that accomplished an analogous effect. An important practical outcome of the music was the flow it imparted to the "ostensibly logical" transitions from scene to scene (which, in terms of musical modulations, are always *wholly* logical, however dissonant they may sound). It is also interesting that Reznicek's approach to the play as a species of Wagnerian "word-tone drama" seems to have stimulated the actors to seek a lightly stylized, musically phrased approach to their delivery.

At this early point in its stage history, however, productions of *A Dream Play* were chiefly concerned with the problem of providing a suitable visual framework for Strindberg's symbolic world. In this respect, both Gade's production concept and his colourful, rather childlike designs for the individual scenes proved to be extremely influential – far more so than, for example, the stunning, Chagall-like decors designed by Knut

11 As part of his purely symbolic scenography for *A Dream Play* in 1916, Svend Gade's design for the second of the scenes in Fingal's Cave depicts the figures of the Daughter and the Poet kneeling in the foreground, watching the blazing apparition of Christ walking on the water.

Ström for a production of the play that he co-directed in Düsseldorf in 1918. Perhaps the most overtly symbolic of Gade's concepts is his sketch for the second of the scenes in Fingal's Cave. In this design, the figures of the Daughter and the Poet are seen kneeling in the foreground, framed by swirling white lines that convey an impression, as Egil Törnqvist observes, "much more like a giant shell or an ear than a cave – although the breaking waves and the wrecked boat help to indicate the realistic aspect."[9] In the dark middle ground of the picture, the blazing apparition of Christ walking on the waves is Gade's expressionistic figuration of the "white glow [that] appears on the water" in the stage directions. Gade first introduced this religious allusion in his design for the Cathedral where the miscarried doctoral ceremony takes place. Here, a spectral, whitish crucifix loomed in the hazy shadows of a church interior suggested by horizontal lines of pews and a soaring forest of vertical organ pipes. This designer's skeletal sets usually combine painted, stylized scenery with three-dimensional pieces isolated in concentrated pools of light – in this instance, the candelabra and announcement board that appear in different guises in earlier scenes of the play. Above all, a sense of the fantastical was present everywhere in Gade's scenography – in his incredibly oversized church organ, in the huge, leafy tree covered with snow that presided over his Fairhaven, in the virtual jungle of hollyhocks that overgrew his strange dream castle.

For a time, it would seem, *A Dream Play* appeared almost inseparable from Gade's spectacular visualization of it. Word of the long-running Berlin premiere spread rapidly, and he was invited to supply a duplicate copy of his scenery for a new Swedish production of the play, mounted by Mauritz Stiller to celebrate the opening of the ultramodern Lorensberg Theatre in Gothenburg on October 27, 1916. As a kind of sales demonstration, he also constructed a scale-model replica of his black-box stage, equipped with electric lighting and machinery for scene changes. Although Gustaf Collijn was prepared to present Gade's rendering of the play at his new Intima teatern in Stockholm, fire destroyed the scenery and the planned production was abandoned. Instead, the designer used his toy-theatre replica to persuade Holger Hofman, manager of the commercial Dagmar Theatre in Copenhagen, to produce "his" mise-en-scène, which opened in the Danish capital on New Year's Day 1917. Gade's autobiography makes no mention of Bernauer's previous production or his own involvement in it, but its description of the Dagmar performance of *A Dream Play* leaves no doubt that the two were identical.[10] Danish audiences approached the strange and unfamiliar play with the reverential awe of churchgoers. "Led by Elith Pio [as the Lawyer], the actors struggled frantically to be a match for the splendour of the scenery," the astringent critic Sven Lange observed at the time.[11]

Hence, while Reinhardt's production at Dramaten in 1921 was to open new perspectives on *A Dream Play*, his work clearly built upon – and commented on – an existing performance tradition for this play. This tradition did not extend beyond the borders of Germany and Scandinavia, however, and the early avant-garde attempts to perform the play elsewhere ended rather unfortunately. At the beginning of 1926 the Provincetown Players, who two years earlier had succeeded with a creditable production of *The Ghost Sonata*, did not fare as well when they staged the American premiere of *A Dream Play* at their tiny theatre in Greenwich Village. In the face of dwindling funds, fading prestige, and inadequate stage facilities, failure was almost certain, particularly with a "faithful" representational approach to the fifteen changes of scene listed in the program. The New York critics dismissed Strindberg and his play, but some praise was reserved for the picturesque chiaroscuro settings created by Cleon Throckmorton. "All of them are of interest and some of them, particularly the Cave of Fingal, with its jagged opening against the purples and greens of the clouds, achieved a striking beauty," Richard Watts, Jr. acknowledged in the *Tribune* (January 21, 1926).

As could be expected, such bourgeois pictorialism was banished conclusively from Antonin Artaud's idiosyncratic attempt to present *A Dream Play* (as *La Songe, ou Jeu des Rêves*) at the Théâtre de l'Avenue in Paris in 1928. There is little doubt that the prophet of the Theatre of Cruelty was sincere in his praise of the work as "one of those model plays whose staging is for a director the crowning achievement of his career. The range of emotions expressed within this one work is infinite . . . In it the highest problems are represented, evoked in a form that is concrete as well as mysterious." He and his troupe, known as the Théâtre Alfred Jarry, were determined to use this experiment "to reintroduce into the theatre the sense, not of life, but of a certain truth that inhabits the deepest strata of the mind. Between real life and the life of dreams there exists a certain interplay of mental associations, relationships between gestures or events that can be translated into actions, which constitute precisely the theatrical reality which the Alfred Jarry Theatre has undertaken to revive." In his simplified, pop-art staging of *A Dream Play*, Artaud's avowed purpose was "to offer nothing to the eyes of the audience which cannot be utilized immediately and as is by the actors. Three-dimensional characters who will be seen moving about amid props, objects, a whole reality that is likewise three-dimensional. The false amid the real: that is the ideal definition of this production."[12]

In theory at least, these ideas might possibly have generated a performance that shed fresh light on the "absurd" qualities of disjuncture and apparent randomness that are to be found in Strindberg's play. The actual production, however, was a noisy fiasco. Jeers and insults, traded freely between stage and auditorium, disrupted the first of its two afternoon showings (June 2). At the second performance one week later, a full-scale riot broke out after Artaud began shouting obscenities at the spectators. Assault on the audience was always a part of Artaudian theory ("In the true theatre a play disturbs the senses' repose," he proclaims in *The Theatre and its Double*). Although the surrealists had become his sworn enemies, one of his chief tactics in his production of *A Dream Play* was the surrealist strategy of introducing totally unexpected and anarchistic movements and objects. For instance, the Lawyer (who, of course, "can never wear clothes for more than one or two days because they stink of other people's crimes") had to bring a ladder on stage and climb to the top of it in order to take down his overcoat from a hanger attached to the

ceiling. "Here's an example of the sort of performance Artaud called for,"
Raymond Rouleau, who played the part of the Lawyer, later recalled in
an interview. "The actor might begin a speech while standing up, but as
he continued to speak he would fall to his knees, then lie down on the
stage, and finally finish the speech on his knees. The audience thought
the actors were ridiculing them."[13] A comment by Tania Balachova, who
played the Daughter of Indra, conveys a more positive sense of artistic
purpose underlying the apparent chaos of Artaud's singular experiment
with Strindberg: "The décor was starkly simplified; it was practically a
bare stage. Yet it was all very real without being naturalistic. Objects
were placed in very strange places; it was pop art in embryo. But this
'pop art' did not give the impression of a music-hall act; Artaud made
it poetic. The lighting was not extreme, and there was no histrionics or
declamation."[14]

Artaud's caricature of *A Dream Play* is remembered now chiefly for
the riots and fistfights it succeeded in provoking. Its weakness was that its
playful anti-bourgeois destructiveness was essentially aesthetic and self-
indulgent, contributing nothing to a fuller understanding of the work
at hand. The contrast with Reinhardt is interesting, because both men
shared so many of the same modernist convictions – about the creative supremacy of the director, the effect of ritual, myth, and symbol
on an audience, the incontestable theatricality of the theatre, and the
distinction that must be made between performance and literary text.
But the conclusive difference between them, as seen in their respective
approaches to *A Dream Play*, lay in Reinhardt's exceptional ability to ana-
lyze and interpret the governing inner rhythm of a text – in this case the
"polyphonic composition" that, as Strindberg insists, is the true essence
of his theatrical symphony.

FROM ALLEGORY TO AUTOBIOGRAPHY: REINHARDT AND
MOLANDER

As a rule, disagreements were noisy and theatres full wherever Max
Reinhardt directed, and his productions of *A Dream Play* in Stockholm
and later in Berlin in 1921 were no exceptions. The Swedish critics
in particular recorded their reservations about the autocratic nature of
his directorial method, the dark tone and pessimistic outcome he gave
the play, and the slow pace and lengthy waits between scenes in his
production. However, no one was inclined to underestimate the virtually mesmeric power of his new mise-en-scène. His successive touring

productions of the post-Inferno plays, beginning with his guest performance of *The Dance of Death* [*Dödsdansen*] at the Royal Opera in Stockholm
in 1915, had already given Swedish audiences a startling and unexpected
introduction to the sheer theatrical power of these plays. As the culmination of this impressive series of Reinhardt interpretations of Strindberg,
his Swedish-language production of *A Dream Play* at Dramaten (October
28, 1921) afforded Stockholm its first opportunity to experience a com-
petent performance of what was still regarded essentially as a reading
drama. No previous production on the national stage had ever attracted
as much popular and critical attention.

Both here and at Reinhardt's Deutsches Theater in Berlin, his interpretation of the play clashed directly – and no doubt deliberately – with
the more optimistic, fairy-tale rendering of it popularized by Bernauer in
Germany and subsequently by Gade in Scandinavia. Reinhardt's earlier
productions of the chamber plays foreshadowed the tone and style of
his *Traumspiel*, an even more provocative contribution to an overall vision of Strindberg in which, to borrow Siegfried Jacobsohn's description,
"a shivering, desperate, shrieking humanity" struggled in an atmosphere
"so distorted, so gloomy, so full of fantastic life and motion, that it might
be Van Gogh's."[15] Almost every reviewer of the Berlin production found
comparisons to make between the respective approaches of Bernauer
and Reinhardt. "For years . . . Bernauer presented the dream as play.
Now at the Deutsches Theater, Reinhardt presents the dream as destiny," Herbert Ihering mused in *Der Tag* (December 15, 1921). "Bernauer
presented variations on a human theme; Reinhardt presents the theme
of humanity. Bernauer gave us complicated Raimund; Reinhardt gives
us Tolstoy." An impressionistic notation in the director's script for the
Stockholm production reveals Reinhardt's own view of *A Dream Play* as
a dark allegory of the human condition: "The purpose of the play is to
depict a rocky sea, darkness, cold misery, but without outrage, without
shedding tears over it, without enlightenment or concession or even sympathy – and yet, in the final outcome, also to inspire deep compassion."[16]
This view produced a mise-en-scène resonant with the feeling of despair
that overwhelms Agnes as the Lawyer's wife and with the tone of anguish
heard in the chorus of dissonant cries that end the Foulstrand scene. This
performance of *A Dream Play* thus made the work a *theatrum mundi*, a vivid
theatrical image of the world and society – in particular the despondent
and strife-torn society of the postwar Weimar Republic.

"Lighting as mise-en-scène," the objective espoused by Per Lindberg,
concisely describes one of the cardinal principles of the Reinhardt

12 Design by Alfred Roller for the Cathedral scene in Max Reinhardt's production of *A Dream Play* at Dramaten in 1921. Like most of Roller's principal designs for the performance, this brooding Gothic interior appeared on stage as a two-dimensional painted backdrop.

method that Lindberg emulated in his own productions. In Reinhardt's staging of *A Dream Play*, the use of spotlights to isolate individual figures and groups in pools of sculpted light on a darkened stage was a technique expressive in itself and also functional as a means of creating a dream-like montage of swiftly changing scenes. (Gade, it will be remembered, used a similar approach and in fact lays claim to its invention in his autobiography.) In the spectral shadow-world of Reinhardt's stage, characters and objects emerged apparition-like out of what Norbert Falk called "nocturnal blackness" (*Berliner Zeitung*, December 14). Cries were heard and watching faces glimpsed in this encroaching primordial darkness, speculatively characterized in one recent commentary as "the unconsciousness from which the lighted fragments of experience emerged."[17]

In fact, however, contemporary reviewers – particularly the Swedish critics familiar with Strindberg's work – were by no means uniformly convinced of either the effectiveness of Reinhardt's strategy or its deeper symbolic significance. "The most important task for the director here is to preserve the play's character as a fleeting dream," Sten Selander writes in *Stockholms Dagblad* (October 29). "Reinhardt can be given credit for not availing himself of a conventional transparent curtain at the front. There must be a more suggestive way to indicate a dream's haziness and unclearness, through lighting, staging, and scenery. But it is this suggestiveness that was generally lacking. There were a couple of nice touches ... but on the whole the scenes, even though fantastical, were alien to the idea of a dream world." This kind of objection to the Stockholm production doubtless arose from Reinhardt's problematic decision to combine his use of expressive, plastic lighting with a succession of two-dimensional painted backdrops, designed by Alfred Roller. Although more stylized and much more emphatic than Grabow's earlier deigns, Roller's sketches are fully as representational in character. Critics were especially displeased by his rendering of the growing castle, which *Aftonbladet* (October 30) called "a hideous cardboard house in cheap architectural taste, with electric lights in the windows ... mounted within a kind of stylized mausoleum of black velvet walls." Much more effective were Roller's moody, rather oppressive images of the theatre corridor where the Officer waits patiently for his Victoria, the Lawyer's office where the clients wait endlessly for justice, and the cathedral where the Lawyer must wait in vain for his degree. The designs for these three consecutive settings, all darkly coloured in shades of brown, green, and black, incorporate the same basic compositional elements – the door

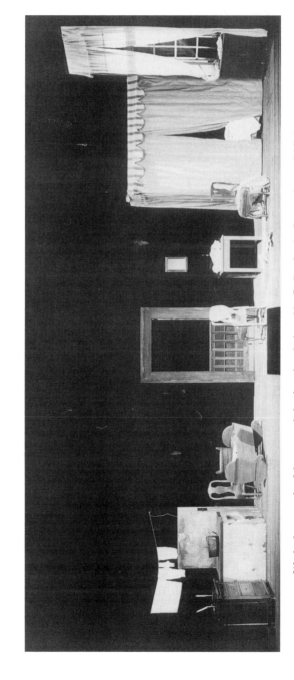

13 Work photograph of the open, skeletal setting designed by Roller for the Lawyer's squalid living quarters.

with the cloverleaf aperture to the right, the linden tree/coat rack/candelabra to the left, and a middle opening leading to an inner space beyond.

On the basis of such sketches alone, however, it is obviously not possible to determine with certainty how a given setting actually looked on the stage. In this regard, the theatre's work photographs showing actual sets in place provide a more accurate (if less attractive) view of specific scenes. Of particular interest are two such photographs that shed light on one of the play's most significant and radical transformations, from the Lawyer's shabby living quarters to the sinister precincts of the quarantine station at Foulstrand. In Roller's open, skeletal setting for the unkempt room shared by Agnes and the Lawyer, the key signifiers of their marital discord pointedly define the otherwise bare space. The dilapidated stove to the left in the picture, with bits of washing strung above it and a chair and rocking cradle beside it, is balanced at the opposite side of the stage by the canopied double bed (obviously unmade) and a window with crooked curtains to torment the Lawyer's sensibility. When Agnes leaves this domestic hell and follows the Officer to the next stage on her journey, part of what she has left behind follows along (as it always does in *A Dream Play*). For the metamorphosis to Foulstrand, Strindberg writes in his stage directions, "the bed with its hangings is transformed into a tent; the iron stove remains." In Roller's rendering of the scene, bed, stove, chairs, and curtained window all reappeared in the new scene, juxtaposed with an immense expressionistic crane and hook to amplify the modestly diabolical implications of Strindberg's "ovens, furnace walls, and piping." On a raised platform at the centre of the composition stands a particularly savage-looking example of the "instruments of torture" Strindberg describes as part of the institution's outdoor gymnasium. The actual manner in which this complex scene change was managed is, in fact, a matter of some doubt. Writing on the basis of her study of Reinhardt's own script, Kela Kvam assumes that the new setting "materialized out of the semi-darkness" as Agnes and the Officer waited on the forestage. However, the stage manager's script of the actual production describes a much less seamless alternative, in which a blackout, a lowered curtain, and the sound of wind and storm all conspired to mask the difficult scene shift.[18] Either way, the critic for *Aftonbladet* voiced a consensus when he pronounced the end result "a far too unruly, obtrusive, and cluttered scene. The characters disappeared behind the foreground of cranes and pipes, while the transparent backdrop of Fairhaven villas twinkling like stars on a Christmas tree

14 In this work photograph of the following scene, set in the sinister quarantine station at Foulstrand, the grimy stove, canopied bed, chairs, and curtained window from the Lawyer's home are still in their places, juxtaposed with a collage of ominous industrial machinery and exercise paraphernalia to suggest the infernal character of the place. In the background, a bleak view of the distant lights of a town seen against a black void replaces the cheerful view of Fairhaven described by Strindberg.

was too banal to be tolerated." Moreover, by disregarding Strindberg's very specific description of Fairhaven as an idyllic vision of summer-house life on the Stockholm archipelago, Roller also blunted the point of the antithesis that this bright and beckoning background was meant to accentuate.

In general, critical complaints about the "foreignness" of Reinhardt's approach were persistent, phrased in different ways but always boiling down to a rejection of the darkness of his interpretation. "Reinhardt achieved what I would call a transposition into German of the whole atmosphere of *A Dream Play*," Johan Danielsson declared in *Social-Demokraten* (October 29). But the "milder chords" and "soulful lyri-cism" that Danielsson and others saw in the play and sought in vain in this performance had indeed been displaced by a much different and harsher tone, heavy with the sense of a virulent human evil and angst that even the Daughter of Indra herself could not overcome. The orchestrated cries and groans of a suffering humanity were heard not only at the end of the Foulstrand scene but from its beginning and, in fact, from the beginning of the play itself, when the Daughter de-scended into the thick black clouds of earth amidst a cacophony of clashing mechanical sounds, discordant music, and human shouting and lamentation.

The expressionistic presence of human strife and suffering in Reinhardt's theatrical allegory acquired a visual as well as an audible dimension. The wall of sorrowing, despairing human faces that ap-pears, according to Strindberg's stage directions, in the closing moments of the play was prepared for in Reinhardt's concept by a comparably hallucinatory vision of "immobile human faces with closed eyes and half-open mouths" that appeared at the beginning, glimpsed through rose-patterned gauze transparencies that masked the growing castle.[19] Wraith-like figures and faces continued to appear and disappear in the surrounding darkness, creating the impression of a watching, waiting chorus. Ejnar Smith's review in *Svenska Dagbladet* provides a persuasive account of Reinhardt's expressive choral strategy:

Beings glided soundlessly forward and away again, phantoms or ghostly pale marionettes. Suddenly the stage space could be filled with these shadows of reality, who struck poses to cover new scene changes. They could be crowded together in compact, deathly silent groups with faces and demeanour united in anxiety, hatred, and wrath. At other times they became compressed figure compositions of contorted limbs, or else diabolical visages staring from the

15 Scene photograph showing the white, staring faces and spectral figures that watch from the darkness during the domestic quarrel between the Lawyer and the Daughter.

walls or creeping forth from the corners to listen anxiously, understandingly, imploringly, or maliciously to the Daughter and her earthly partner, the Lawyer, when hatred and evil words infect their home.

As this comment suggests, the clients who crowd about the Lawyer's office and later lurk outside the door of his private quarters became in this performance an ambiguous chorus of needy suppliants and menacing furies. Their "white, staring, convulsively contorted faces" seemed to Bo Bergman to form "a visionary background and a silent accompaniment" to the situation. "The Rembrandt darkness enveloping the stage, from which these shadows of crime and suffering streamed, was also splendidly conceived and realized" (*Dagens Nyheter*). The marriage scene in the Lawyer's home, which opened the second act of Reinhardt's compact three-act stage version of the play, was a pivotal episode in his mise-en-scène, centred on the crucial moment when the Daughter experiences the full human despair of her mortal persona. In Jessie Wessel's performance of the role, the growing sense of entrapment precipitated by Kristin's sealing up of the window was intensified by the watching presence of disembodied, skull-like faces that appeared in the black drapes in the background during the course of her harrowing confrontation with Gustaf Molander's weary, perpetually tormented Lawyer. These expressionistic apparitions were intermittent, marking the ebb and flow of the domestic combat:[20]

DAUGHTER But what shall we eat? Fish? You hate fish.
   (*Faces visible in the drapes*)
LAWYER And it's expensive.
DAUGHTER This is harder than I thought.
LAWYER (*Kindly*) You see how hard it is! . . . And the child who should be our bond and blessing . . . becomes our undoing. (*The faces disappear*)

As the anger and discord again intensified, the watching faces reappeared:

DAUGHTER I think I'm beginning to hate you after this!
LAWYER Then woe to us! . . . But let us beware of hatred. I promise I shall never mention untidiness again . . . even though it is a torment for me. (*Faces visible in the drapes*)
DAUGHTER And I shall eat cabbage, even though it nauseates me.
LAWYER A life of torment together, then! One's pleasure is the other's pain.

[. . .]

DAUGHTER Yes. But let us for God's sake avoid the rocks, now that we know them so well! (*The faces disappear*)

Only a few moments later, her admission that she has burned her husband's newspaper unleashes a fresh outburst of indignation from the
Lawyer, causing the faces to reappear and the shadowy figures in the
doorway to advance toward the terrified Daughter:

DAUGHTER Now smile! . . . I burned it because it ridiculed all that is sacred
    to me.
LAWYER And that is not sacred to me! . . . I see.
    (*All forward to the Daughter, and faces in the drapes*)
    Oh, I shall smile, I shall smile so my molars show . . . I'll be humane, and keep
    my opinions to myself, and say yes to everything, and pussyfoot around and
    pretend. [. . .] Agnes, this is simply impossible.
DAUGHTER Yes, it is. (*All move backward again*)

A moment later, just before being rescued from her confinement by Ivar
Nilsson's wildly exuberant Officer ("The world is mine! All roads stand
open to me"), Wessel's Daughter touched the lowest and bitterest point
on her journey: "*She bows her head in mute despair.*"
    Reinhardt's ghostly chorus reappeared both as groaning inmates of the
quarantine station and as ballroom dancers at Fairhaven, but this repeti-
tiveness seemed to some critics to overdo and thereby dissipate the effect
of this device. "When the spooks become so domesticated that we no
longer notice them, then their purpose miscarries," Mia Leche observed
in *Göteborgs Handelstidning* (October 31). The nightmarish mood evoked in
Reinhardt's second act by these figurations of universal suffering was also
gradually displaced in his short final movement by a milder, more conciliatory tone. Reinhardt's radical cutting and transposing of the play's
last four scenes was an essential element in this change. The scene with
the Coal-Heavers on the Mediterranean beach, which opened the third
act of his production, led not to Fingal's Cave but directly back to the
theatre corridor, where another form of social discontent is displayed
when the chorus of All the Righteous Ones denounces the Daughter
after the opening of the cloverleaf door reveals nothing (or at least nothing that is visible to the human eye). This strident public scene of the
battling Deans and the near-lynching of the Daughter by the angry mob
was then followed and counterbalanced in Reinhardt's performance by
the private, contemplative scene in Fingal's Cave, played in a shadowy
liminal space between earth and heaven – in fact the very wilderness
"where no one can hear or see us," to which the Daughter invites the
Poet in Strindberg's text. By moving some of their prose dialogue about
the wrecked ship back to their previous scene in the theatre corridor,

Reinhardt distilled the Fingal's Cave episode into a brief, intensely lyrical duet between the Poet (Uno Henning) and the goddess. His object was obviously to create a clearer and less sudden tonal transition to the mystical ritual of sacrifice and atonement that ends the play.

Despite his efforts, however, critical opposition to Reinhardt's handling of the final scene was strong. For one thing, Jessie Wessel – whom some critics had found too stilted and declamatory as Agnes – now seemed at the end to lack the heightened poetic tone that her resumption of divinity calls for. "From the scenes with the Poet, Indra's Daughter begins to lay aside her mortal guise, her speech becomes rhythmic – but during this free interplay of rhythms the director let the actress retain the same anxious tone as before," complained Ejnar Smith, who maintained that the Daughter's final scene required "more rhetoric, a more solemn and heightened delivery" to command renewed attention on the part of "the weary listeners." More general were the critical objections to the actual staging of the Daughter's leavetaking. Reciting her parting words to the Poet to music, she stepped onto the low altar of burning logs on which all the other characters in the play had laid their offerings. Then, in Mia Leche's sarcastic account, she "sank into the ground through a trap while the castle shone in a Bengal light like the closing ballet in a music-hall show." (In fairness to Reinhardt, it might be noted that this controversial conclusion corresponded directly to the Daughter's own description of what would happen to her. In Fingal's Cave, in answer to the Poet's question, she replies that she will return to heaven only after "I have burned this mortal coil away, for not all the water in the world can cleanse me.")

No chrysanthemum bloomed atop the growing castle in Reinhardt's production, and the Swedish critics found the perceived pessimism of his counter-image of Indra's Daughter descending into the flames difficult to accept. Their reviews reflect a shared dismay at Reinhardt's oppressively nightmarish reinterpretation of *A Dream Play*. Although the production undeniably possessed "admirable details," Bo Bergman conceded, "something much too harsh and declamatory ruptured the dreamlike tone." By contrast, postwar audiences and critics in Berlin, for whom the appeal of Bernauer's fairy-tale treatment of the play had faded, found Reinhardt's nightmare vision of human suffering and anguish a truer mirror of a daily existence overshadowed by poverty, labour unrest, political turmoil, and the chaos of military defeat.

In Reinhardt's new *Traumspiel* at his Deutsches Theater, distinguished by the tightly knit ensemble playing for which his German company was

16 Work photograph of the final setting in the Reinhardt production, showing Roller's version of the Growing Castle and the controversial altar of logs that became a flaming pyre mounted by the Daughter after her leavetaking.

renowned, the unevenness that had arisen from working with unfamiliar actors in a foreign language also disappeared. Helene Thimig's portrayal of Indra's Daughter and Eugen Klöpfer's remarkable refiguration of the Lawyer's role shared the focus of attention in the Berlin reviews. Dressed "in the long, crumpled coat of the poorhouse solicitor," the strange figure that Klöpfer drew seemed to Paul Fechter "a mixture of a man from the lower depths and a ghost." His performance became the physical embodiment of the leitmotif of human wretchedness that unified Reinhardt's interpretation. Fechter describes him in *Deutsche Allgemeine Zeitung* (December 14) as "a Christ figure from the realm of the neediest, with huge, powerless hands protruding from sleeves too short for him." As his mortal companion, Helene Thimig's blond, vulnerable Agnes was, in Fechter's words, "from the outset a suffering human being, at least a fellow sufferer with the others." Thimig (Reinhardt's wife and the sister of Hermann Thimig, who played the Officer) was the subdued spiritual centre of the production, closer in this respect to Harriet Bosse's performance of the role than to the leading-ladylike style of Jessie Wessel and Irene Triesch. There was no elaborate descent from a star-filled heaven, as there had been with Triesch and Wessel. Instead, Thimig simply stepped out of the impenetrable darkness into a blazing pool of white light at the beginning of the play. "Standing silently in the light, with her black dress and blond hair, she visibly seemed to assume the mantle of all human suffering, [like] a Nazarene mother of sorrows," Monty Jacobs wrote in *Vossische Zeitung* (December 14).

A freer sense of creative experimentation also made itself felt in the Berlin performance. Inconceivable under the constrictions of his guest production in Stockholm was Reinhardt's casting of Werner Krauss, a famous character actor and master of disguises, in no fewer than five different roles. Krauss turned up first in the theatre corridor as the officious policeman ("a larger-than-life dream policeman") who prohibits the opening of the cloverleaf door. Next he appeared in Foulstrand as a young, blond, rotund Quarantine Master in a black mask. Then he was the savage schoolmaster who intimidates the bewildered Officer – "massive, heavy, with unruly, whitened hair, the personification of an anxiety nightmare," as Fechter saw him. Later he materialized on the beach at the Riviera as a gruff, sooty-black coal-heaver. Finally, this shape-changer returned once more as the indignant Dean of Law who threatens the Daughter with stoning. Krauss' reappearances – which were always anticipated by the audience, yet always a surprise – thus comprised an integral part of the metamorphic fabric of the dream. In his prefatory note to the play, Strindberg emphasizes that its characters split, double, evaporate, and coalesce. In this sense, as Evert Sprinchorn argues, doubling "is not an economic desideratum in this play; it is an essential part of its method. In the ideal production, there would be not fifty actors but two: one man, one woman, who would fragment themselves."[21] (At least one practical demonstration of Sprinchorn's somewhat odd suggestion was a production given at the Teatro de la Casa de la Paz in Mexico City in 1966, in which Carlos Ancira played all the male parts while Maria Teresa Rivas played all the female ones.) In this context, then, Reinhardt's production in Berlin holds special significance as the first of many attempts to explore this crucial aspect of performing *A Dream Play*.

In this production in general, more consistently than in his Stockholm version, Reinhardt used the transformation and mutation of scenes, physical objects, and figure compositions to create the sense of a rapidly flowing stream of dream images. In Paul Fechter's words, "he built an unreal world of light coming from nocturnal darkness, out of which he allowed image after image to develop." To accomplish this and to eliminate the scenographic awkwardness that sometimes marred the Stockholm performance, he dispensed altogether with Roller's fixed, pictorialized settings, replacing them with fewer, more impressionistic background images, designed by Franz Dworsky. Dworsky's preliminary sketches employ suggestion rather than depiction to achieve their purpose. They are chiaroscuro mood studies of sharply lighted windows and shadowy facades for the castle and the theatre corridor, a stained-glass window and illuminated organ pipes for the cathedral, gleaming, jagged stalactites against a black ground to evoke Fingal's Cave.[22] Liberated from the sequential depiction of localities imposed by Roller's conventional scenography, Reinhardt now used the blurred and shadowy outlines of Dworsky's phantom castle as his principal unifying image, enveloped in a perpetual darkness from which characters and scenes emerged in hallucinatory fashion. Within the castle, as it were, other "places" were revealed – the corridor, the church, the cave – but it was primarily the expressionistic use of light carved out of darkness that created space for the action and maintained the flow of fantastical images.

From its expressive staging and choreographed mass scenes to the futuristic musical score provided by the Bulgarian composer Pantscho Wladigeroff, every component of Reinhardt's mise-en-scène for *A Dream Play* contributed to the unified emotional impression of what he calls in a script note "the senseless chaos of an aggressive, murderous, and dying world."[23] As we have already begun to see, however, it was this nihilistic view of Strindberg that led to the growing repudiation, particularly in Sweden, of what Olof Molander termed "German Reinhardt-inspired romantic expressionism." Strindberg himself makes it plain enough in his foreword that his play is not a discourse on the chaos and terribleness of life; its subject is the *dream* that causes us to recognize both life's terribleness and also its impermanent, illusory nature. "But when the torture is at its worst," Strindberg writes, "the sufferer awakens and is reconciled with reality – which, however painful it can be, is at that moment a joy when compared to the torment of the dream." This lucid undertone of reconciliation and consolation in Strindberg's writing, so often absent in the German *Schrei* versions of his post-Inferno plays, became the hallmark of Molander's consciously revisionist revival of *A Dream Play* at Dramaten in 1935, exactly fourteen years after Reinhardt's guest production of it on the same stage. Differences between the approaches of these two directors were numerous and fundamental, but on one point they were in full agreement – the intrinsic performability of Strindberg's theatre poetry.

Reality and dream seemed to merge in Molander's work into what some referred to as his surrealism. "Here one is in the midst of the dream, yet it seems to us at the same time more real than reality, uglier, more unsettling, more bitter, more beautiful. It is a condensed reality," Bo Bergman, the only critic who had reviewed both Reinhardt's revival and the world premiere of the play, observed in *Dagens Nyheter* (October 26, 1935). The "condensed reality" to which this comment refers was grounded, precisely as Martin Lamm's critical interpretations of Strindberg's plays were grounded, in autobiography, in the identification of actual places and events in the playwright's life that lie encoded in his writing. "*A Dream Play* is perhaps the most autobiographical of all of Strindberg's dramas, although until now this has hardly been recognized," Molander told *Dagens Nyheter* (October 24) before the opening, adding that he had found "a line – Strindberg's own life-line" in the play, whose principal male characters were "all three none other than Strindberg himself."

As Molander's remark suggests, the spine of his interpretation was the identification of the Dreamer, in all three of his voices, with the playwright himself. His presence was felt in the young, eternally expectant Officer created by Lars Hanson, in the mature Lawyer (Gabriel Alw) whose bearded, careworn face bespoke the human pain in which he deals, and especially in Ivar Kåge's aging Poet who, actually made up to resemble Strindberg, sat at the feet of the Daughter of Indra – his muse and his own creation – to learn of the interchangeability of poetry and dream. The Poet in Reinhardt's version had – particularly in the Stockholm production – been a comparatively weak and insignificant character, viewed on the same plane as all the other examples of suffering humanity. By contrast, Molander presented him as the personification of the omniscient consciousness described in the author's foreword, the artist-dreamer for whom "there are no secrets, no contradictions, no scruples, no law." As a result, this suggestion of a Strindberg persona, standing both within the play and outside of it, introduced a new quality of reflective irony that mitigated the harshness of Reinhardt's nightmare vision of life. Kåge's sensitive, layered characterization of the Poet revealed, in Grevenius' words, "a hearty and exuberant cordiality beneath which one seemed to sense the rapid pulse of doubt" (*Stockholms Tidningen*, October 26).

In the role of the Daughter of Indra, Tora Teje was a majestic, meditative figure in black who likewise often seemed to stand outside the action, as if watching a play-within-the-play being enacted for her. Her normally powerful, passionate vocal delivery was moderated to convey what Anders Österling described as "a calm, melancholy conviction that silences all objections" (*Svenska Dagbladet*, October 26). In turn, her sympathetic, watching presence added to the strongly oneiric dimension that Molander imparted to the moments of profoundest ignominy in the play, notably the humiliation of the Lawyer at the Degree Ceremony and the agony of the Officer at the hands of the Schoolmaster. In the former scene, after bestowing a crown of thorns on Alw's Lawyer ("Come, I'll give you a wreath – one that will become you"), Teje sat quietly at his feet as he raised his arms, one after the other, in the form of an invisible cross to which he was being "nailed' (to the actual sound of a spike being driven). With the Daughter as audience and the Lawyer as actor-demonstrator, his pain was thus transposed into a new and more universalized dream-image of vicarious suffering.

An analogous effect was achieved in the scene in which the Officer finds himself seated on the school-bench again, obliged to relearn old forgotten lessons and repeat old mistakes. Trapped in a nightmare of recurrences, he also became both the dreamer and the player in a dream sequence watched by the Daughter. "In this scene Lars Hanson expressed a *wonderment* that came from the depths of his spirit," Vagn Børge later recalled. "Surprise became, all at once, uneasiness, fear, and touching helplessness. The lines were spoken as if by a sleepwalker, seeking clarification because he is half aware that he is dreaming."[24] When the

Molander production of *A Dream Play* visited Copenhagen on tour, the noted Danish critic Frederik Schyberg described Hanson's Officer as "a marionette of dreams, sorrow, and unhappiness, his face frozen in an unforgettable mixture of eagerness and pained surprise."[25] It was precisely this extraordinary mimic expressiveness that made Hanson the ideal Strindberg actor, capable of exploiting to the fullest the ironic doubleness of a scene in which, as Richard Bark puts it, "he is both dreamer and dream figure." To clarify his point, Bark cites an interesting letter from Molander, written about one of his later revivals of the play but fully as applicable to the 1935 production: "The school dream is thus a play-within-the-play, *performed for the Daughter*. Narrated by the Officer! . . . It is his nightmare that arouses her empathy."[26]

Impressive as these individual acting performances were, however, it was the powerful overall effect of Molander's mise-en-scène for *A Dream Play* that made this production so seminal. Its basic style, which he himself characterized as "hyperrealistic," was shaped by his determination to anchor the play firmly in the matter-of-fact reality of Strindberg's personal experiences, unencumbered by what he regarded as the gratuitous shock effects introduced by Reinhardt. "For Strindberg life was such, so filled with misery, that it is best to depict its variations by just taking it as it is," he observed in the pre-production interview with *Dagens Nyheter*. "We believe quite simply that he dreamed the dream pictures with incredible reality. So we are performing the play completely realistically . . . and I assure those who crave it that it will still be scary enough; when we show the old Dr. Zander machines [the outdoor physiotherapy equipment that caught Strindberg's eye at the baths in Furusund and gave him the idea for the grotesque open-air gymnasium in the Foulstrand scene], these instruments of torture will be fully as terrifying as the weird theatre machines displayed by Reinhardt in his day."

Sven Erik Skawonius designed a rhythmic, oneiric flow of fragmentary settings for the production, each built up of selected bits of sharply etched reality. These skeletal sets were in turn collated with a succession of stylized back projections, created on the basis of sketches by the modernist painter Isaac Grünewald, whose commissioned set designs had been rejected by Molander as inappropriately expressionist. Skawonius' shadowy dream images were predominantly black and white, each with a strongly lighted focus – a table and chair, an announcement board with hymn numbers for the cathedral scene, the omnipresent cloverleaf door in varying contexts, and so on. The reiteration of certain objects also served to link scenes in a new and unexpected way, as when the

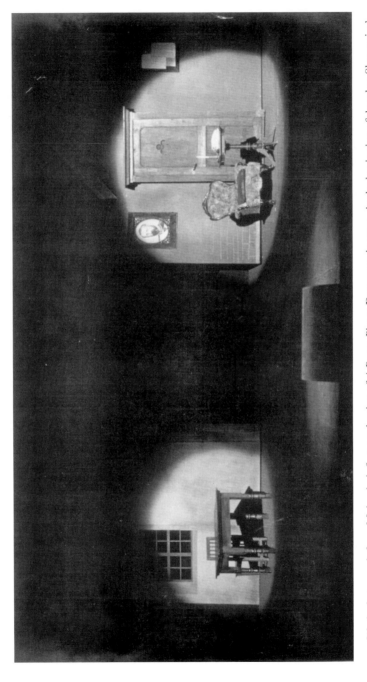

17 Work photograph from Molander's first production of *A Dream Play* at Dramaten in 1935. At the beginning of the play, Skawonius' divided stage used spotlights to isolate and transpose (left) the simple table at which the Officer sits inside the Castle and (right) the homely sitting room where he and Agnes meet his parents.

armchair and sewing table used for the domestic scene with the Mother and Father of the Officer turned up again, in exactly the same position, in the unhappy home that Agnes shares with the Lawyer. Beyond these minimalist settings one saw at times only a background of impenetrable darkness. At other times, however, Grünewald's projected visions filled the cyclorama with suggestive period glimpses of Stockholm and its surroundings – the summer-house landscape of the archipelago, the old Royal Theatre, and, at the beginning and the end of the play, stylized images of the red Horse Guard barracks that Strindberg saw from his window and called the Growing Castle. Grevenius describes the Theatre Corridor, for example, as "a concentrated picture of idyllic nineteenth-century Stockholm . . . which with dreamlike logic is both an interior and an exterior at one and the same time. Blue monk's-hood plants around Molin's fountain, Jacob's Church as a gilded vision, a fragment of the old opera house." Particularly to the Swedish audiences of the day, these allusions to a recognizable time and place seemed to shed an entirely new light on Strindberg's play. "This was precisely what was lacking in Reinhardt, and the resulting impression was therefore more chaotic and disconcerting than it ought to have been for Strindberg's own country-men," Österling argued in *Svenska Dagbladet*, "Now, Grünewald's imagi-native projections give us the right reminder of the underlying reality of the scenes."

The dichotomic character of the scenography established an irony that suited Strindberg's purposes perfectly, not least in the Foulstrand/Fairhaven sequence, where the language of disjuncture is the operative medium. The oppressive confines of Foulstrand and its Quarantine Sta-tion were suggested very simply: a diagonal bit of tiled wall with an iron gate and an open tent with the strange exercise machines stood at ei-ther side of the stage on small revolving turntables. In the background, Grünewald's picture-postcard view of Fairhaven ("a vision of Swedish villas and greenery and sails on the water," as Österling put it) beckoned mockingly from across the strait. Then, after lowering the curtain and giving the two revolves half a turn, the foreground became Fairhaven in winter. The clapboard wall of the schoolroom and a corner of an open-air dance pavilion appeared in place of the tiled wall and the tent. Everything – even the lid of Ugly Edith's piano – was covered with a light blanket of snow, while in the background loomed the sinister contours of Grünewald's Foulstrand, a barren landscape of deformed trees and snowy drifts.

18 Work photograph of the Skawonius setting for Foulstrand and its Quarantine Station. The upper part of the photo is the festive background projection of Fairhaven drawn by Isaac Grünewald. By turning the two small revolves, the foreground was quickly transformed from one realm to the other.

Molander's mise-en-scène divided the stage space into three distinct planes, including a raised structure at the back, used mainly for the grotesque funereal procession at the Degree Ceremony and for the final *défilé*, and a shallow forestage one step below the level of the main playing area. Molander incorporated a similar step-down forestage in his subsequent production of *To Damascus* as a means of framing the action, but here the device was used to produce a very different kind of effect. Grevenius was particularly impressed by the "bold and clever use of the forestage when figures seemed to step out into the auditorium, without thereby disrupting the sense of a dividing line." From time to time, as this comment suggests, one or another of the four principal characters – the Officer, the Lawyer, the Poet, and the Daughter – moved to the forestage area to watch the action, becoming, as it were, a spectator of the waking dream in which he or she also played a role. The director's script indicates that the black-masked Quarantine Master was also given access to this liminal space during the Foulstrand sequence, when he joined the Daughter and the Officer on the forestage as a spectator and interpreter of the events in his strange domain.[27]

This use of these watching characters reinforced a prevailing atmosphere of theatre-in-the-theatre that was nowhere more emphatic than in the final beats of action in Molander's first production of *A Dream Play*. Near the end of the Daughter's encounter with the angry mob of "right-thinking people," the setting for the Theatre Corridor was hoisted up out of sight, leaving her last bitter domestic confrontation with the Lawyer to be played out on a bare stage against a black background. As their quarrel about "life's little tribulations" ended, the stage was plunged into darkness. When the light returned, virtually the entire cast had assembled to lay their various emblems of human suffering upon a simple altar that had been erected on the raised platform at the back. Beyond the platform, Grünewald's second image of the now-completed Flowering Castle filled the cyclorama. Molander's script calls for no fewer than twenty different characters to swell the procession, which moved (as did the analogous procession at the Degree Ceremony) to the strains of Chopin's "Funeral March." Unlike the cheerless conclusion to Reinhardt's *Traumspiel*, in which the descent of Indra's Daughter into the flames had been followed by the sound and music of human misery and a wall of pale human faces peering through clouds of smoke, the burning of the castle was reduced in Molander's version to a hint of red back lighting that changed to pure blue as the Daughter disappeared and the castle projection vanished. It was replaced on the cyclorama by a jumbled photographic collage of faces as the Poet with Strindberg's countenance remained ("as their spokesperson," Grevenius suggested) standing and watching, alone on the deserted stage. As a kind of mystical benediction, a cross rose above the small altar in the background, bearing the inscription that Strindberg had chosen for his own grave: Ave crux spes unica ("Hail, O Cross, our only hope"). Although a great deal changed in Molander's subsequent revivals of *A Dream Play*, the interpolation of religious (specifically Christian) symbolism was to remain a recurrent element in all of them.

This ongoing exploration of *A Dream Play* through production after production may justly be regarded as the central achievement of Molander's long and varied directing career. He staged his seventh and last revival of the play at Det Norske Teatret in Oslo in 1965, the year before his death. But for Molander, no production of this work was ever quite the ideal one. "I will never get the chance to mount *A Dream Play* in the way I would like," he told an interviewer in 1965. "The resources, not least on the acting level, which this Strindbergian masterpiece requires in order to, in my opinion, come even close to doing it justice are so colossal that no theatre has them at its disposal."[28]

Although the surrealistic or "hyperrealistic" style that he and Skawonius had introduced in the 1935 premiere remained the hallmark of Molander's subsequent revivals, the precise character of that style varied considerably from one production of *A Dream Play* to another. For instance, when he restaged the play at the Danish Royal Theatre in Copenhagen in 1940, his script indicates the adoption of a virtually operatic mode of musical accompaniment that involved an extremely complex pattern of musical cues. Most of the prologue was spoken to music from Ravel's *Daphnis et Chloé*, while during the remainder of the action one heard an almost continuous symphonic accompaniment, consisting of an orchestral potpourri comprised of a Beethoven quartet, the Chopin Funeral March, Ravel's *Daphnis* and his colourful orchestral suite *Rapsodie espagnole*, Bach's *Toccata con fuga* No. 10 (Strindberg's choice), a little Mozart, and much more.

For the Copenhagen production (where he was credited with the scenography as well), Molander also chose to abandon the localized views of Strindberg's Stockholm that had figured prominently in his initial approach to the play. In their place, Grevenius writes, he "worked with purely photographic projections, neutral cityscapes, summer villas in grey and white, the special colour of dreams, according to the experts. But the decorative element remained the period costuming with its lively, realistic colour values."[29] The use of similarly neutral back projections in a bleached grey-and-white ("filmic") tone became even more pronounced when Molander next staged the play at the Malmö City Theatre in 1947. Here, the stage designs created by Martin Ahlbom acquired a much hazier, "dreamier" character, due in part to the reduced resolution of the projections on the unusually wide Malmö stage. To counteract the sense of a barrier between this immense stage and the auditorium, Ahlbom also built stairs down from its elliptical apron, thereby allowing certain characters (the Poet, the Blind Man) to make their entrances from that angle. In the controversial closing scene, in which the altar was once more replaced by a pile of logs upon which the characters laid their offerings, a heavy wooden cross bearing the Strindbergian epitaph again appeared in the background – to which even a loyal admirer like Grevenius felt obliged to take exception: "As a picture it is powerful. But it is the wrong closing image for *A Dream Play*, which is hardly a Christian drama but builds instead on religious feelings of a more universal kind."[30]

Later in 1947 at the Gothenburg City Theatre, Molander's fourth approach to *A Dream Play* suddenly assumed a different, darker tone closer to Reinhardt's, permeated by a postwar sense of despair and defiance. The bearing force in this interpretation was now the psychologically intense and embittered portrait of the Lawyer created by Anders Ek, whose humiliation, crowning with thorns, and symbolic crucifixion at the Degree Ceremony in the cathedral became the most harrowing and representative experience in the drama. This time projections were eliminated entirely, and Molander and his designer, Carl-Johan Ström, experimented instead with solid, plastic elements. The Growing Castle was thus a three-dimensional miniature of the Horse Guard barracks, resting on piles of straw and flanked by immense, multi-coloured hollyhocks. In the closing scene, flames licked at its roof but no faces appeared in the empty windows. As the castle sank noiselessly into the earth, a Molander cross again appeared in the background – this time, however, not the marker from Strindberg's grave but a high, slender silhouette seen against a fiery red horizon, rising above the blackened ruins of a bombed-out city. In the foreground stage centre stood the heavy, solitary figure of the Poet (Sven Miliander) with his sombre Strindberg countenance.

Although Molander was apparently dissatisfied that "only" forty-three rehearsals were held for his final production of *A Dream Play*, seen at Det Norske Teatret in Oslo in 1965, he later conceded in a radio interview that he regarded this version as his best. His collaborator on this occasion was Arne Walentin, one of Norway's foremost stage designers. In his preliminary correspondence with him, Molander asked his scenographer whether a more simplified and unified production concept could not be achieved by making "one composition out of all the sets, with a platform serving as mid-axis, around which chairs, tables, doors, wardrobe etc. are placed." His aim was "to clear away everything that is superfluous." Projections could be used to provide "a sustained backdrop, 'the description of the atmosphere in the atmosphere,' so to speak. But what we place on the stage can be more ephemeral."[31] Walentin responded with design work that made effective use of the limited stage facilities at his disposal. This in turn stimulated Molander to approach the play in a new way, with (in the designer's words) "the reality of the dream-world" as his guide. A few key bits of scenery – notably an announcement

19 The simplified unit setting designed by Arne Walentin for Molander's final production of *A Dream Play* at Det Norske Teatret in Oslo in 1965. Here, a background projection of decaying slums provides the atmosphere for the scenes with the Lawyer.

board and the door with the cloverleaf pattern – were kept on the stage throughout the action. Other linking objects were transmogrified, as it were, from one thing into another, as when the linden tree that blooms and withers outside the Theatre Corridor became (as it has frequently done in performance) first a coat rack in the Lawyer's office and then a candlestand in the Cathedral scene. A sense of place and atmosphere was evoked chiefly by Walentin's back projections, which ranged in style from a stark photographic image of decaying slums in the scenes with the Lawyer to a shimmering vision of a rose window and organ pipes for the macabre Degree Ceremony in the cathedral.

One of the most notable changes in this later revival was Molander's new decision to eliminate the prologue in heaven altogether. Already in his 1935 production, he had been determined to avoid staging the descent of Indra's Daughter as a theatrical spectacle, preferring instead to let the opening exchange between her and the god Indra be heard but not seen, spoken behind a decorative front curtain depicting stylized clouds. By the end of his career, however, even this choice seemed wrong. Rut Tellefsen, who played the role of the Daughter in the Oslo production, explained in an interview that "he found it more interesting and challenging to suggest the Daughter's divinity scene by scene than to state it clearly in advance." Her opening scene with the Glazier, played on a bare stage in front of a colourful, highly stylized Flowering Castle, was completely dreamlike. Then, Tellefsen explains, once having entered the castle, the characters "were considered to be in life-on-earth and their speech and movements ceased to be dreamlike and became realistic."[32] A correspondingly spare closing scene also dispensed with the more overt religious and autobiographical allusions of the earlier productions. A blue doorframe stood on an otherwise empty stage, beyond which one saw a projected image of the Flowering Castle. Through this suggestive doorway the characters passed in procession as they spoke their final lines. The castle projection turned a fiery red and then faded from the cyclorama, to be replaced by the sorrowful face of a woman whose image was repeated over and over until it filled the entire background. This single face, Molander was now persuaded, was enough to signify the play's true subject, the suffering of all humanity.

ACTORS IN AN EMPTY SPACE

The new, simpler style apparent in Molander's final revival of *A Dream Play* reflected the broader forces of change and renewal that had been set in motion by Ingmar Bergman's early productions of Strindberg in the 1950s. Beginning with his first major Strindberg production, a radically simplified and dematerialized stage version of *The Crown-Bride* [*Kronbruden*] presented on the main stage of the Malmö City Theatre in 1952, Bergman adopted an approach that implicitly challenged accepted ideas and conventions of Strindberg performance enshrined by the work of such predecessors as Molander and Lindberg. The rehearsal period for *The Crown-Bride* became, in effect, an early but critical turning point in Bergman's general development as a stage director. "One of the reasons I have dispensed more and more with scenery is because I believe that every stagehand on the stage, every use of the curtain, every raising and lowering of settings is a disruptive occurrence," he later recalled in an interview. "I thought about this very intensively while I was rehearsing the closing scenes for *The Crown-Bride*. Everyone went around in rehearsal clothes and we had only rehearsal light. It struck me that absolutely no more was needed, no lighting was needed, nothing was needed – nothing more than the performer [*artiste*]. It is that simple."[33]

Underlying this observation is Bergman's belief in the force of suggestion, the single most important link between his film work and his theatre

work. Persistently, his films refuse to allow the spectator to become lost
in the details of an outer reality. "I just want you to sit down and look at
the human faces," he says simply – adding: "if there is too much going
on in the background . . . if the lighting is too realistic, the face is lost."[34]
In theatrical terms, his emphasis on a neutral, uncluttered performance
space is likewise intended to produce an enriched concentration and
emotional intensification, both on the part of the actor and on the part
of the spectator. In the specific instance of *The Crown-Bride*, he categori-
cally eliminated the elements of folklore, fairy tale, and picturesque local
colour that had hitherto (most recently in Molander's production of the
play at Dramaten three years earlier) seemed indispensable to directors
and critics of this ambiguous post-Inferno work. In doing so, he deliberately shifted the focus of interest from the external to the internal, from a
potentially spectacular visual display to the inner drama of the troubled
and defiant Kersti, the peasant girl who drowns her baby in order to
marry her lover as a "crown" (i.e., virgin) bride. "Bergman has by and
large eliminated the realistic elements," Per Erik Wahlund observed in
Svenska Dagbladet (November 15, 1952). "In his hands, the latent dream-
play technique is laid bare and accentuated by the shadowy half-light
and a radically stylized décor."

   In the first scenes of the production, Per Falk's stage settings still incorporated realistic details that evoked a sense of specific and very sinister
locations in what a program note called "a world where the powers
hold sway and a dreaded God drives human beings to penance and destruction." As the performance progressed, however, the depth of the
stage was increased, and it was gradually and deliberately stripped of
all objects and details as the action moved toward Kersti's penance, humiliation, and death. The fateful bridal procession, during which she is
forced to confess her perfidy and forfeit her crown, was choreographed
(to music from Ture Rangström's opera on the subject) on a virtually
bare and sombre stage illuminated only by what Wahlund describes as
"the moon's gigantic, flame-coloured stratospheric balloon in the background." The technically daunting climax, in which Kersti attempts to
cross the treacherous ice of Krummedikke Lake on her way to church
to perform public penance, became the most impressive achievement of
Bergman's suggestively simplified mise-en-scène. The mill folk and the
outsiders, the feuding parties for whose sake the girl becomes a divine sacrifice for reconciliation, clashed and fought with oars on a storm-lashed
stretch of lake ice that was nothing more or less than the bare floor
of the stage itself, opened up to its full spectacular width of thirty-six

meters (117 feet). Using only this immense space and the chiaroscuro effects that are obtained when darkness is penetrated by scattered shafts of light, Bergman literally conjured forth what Ebbe Linde described in *Dagens Nyheter* (November 15) as "a limitless ice field with a swirling snowstorm coming toward us." In this dark, distinctly antipastoral rendering of *The Crown-Bride*, it was only in the closing sequence, when the warring factions are reconciled and the sunken church rises (like a Flowering Castle) to signify peace in Dalecarlia and on earth, that the director finally resolved and reaffirmed the major tonic chord of redemption in Strindberg's work.

Bergman's growing preoccupation at this time with an elimination of external detail and a consequent tightening of focus on the presence of the actor manifested itself in a rather different way in his unorthodox production of *Erik XIV* in 1956. Although Ebbe Linde commented in *Dagens Nyheter* (December 8) that "what must have fascinated Ingmar Bergman were the possibilities of making something spectacular out of a text that has so often been regarded as virtually unplayable," it is well to understand the nature of the "spectacular" element in this case. Wahlund's review of the Bergman production in *Svenska Dagbladet* (December 8) made a point of stressing parallels between it and the imposing revival of this play staged by Alf Sjöberg at Dramaten in 1950, in which a superb cast featured Ulf Palme as Erik and Lars Hanson as his scheming procurator Göran Persson. Sjöberg, whose extensive and very influential work with Strindberg was otherwise almost exclusively concentrated on the pre-Inferno plays, adopted a visually exciting epic style for *Erik XIV* that was to remain typical of his epoch-making productions of Shakespeare in the fifties and sixties. Stellan Mörner designed a soaring "Shakespearean" décor on three levels, consisting of a permanent structure of platforms, stairs, ramparts, and a drawbridge. Within this silhouetted framework, individual elements – a ship, a gate, a bit of furniture, and so on – were deftly introduced to suggest the seven successive interiors and exteriors described by Strindberg in his stage directions. "We want to create productions with no other resources than the simplest, the poorest," Sjöberg declared in a manifesto published at this time in *Prisma* (1950). "The ideal stage is and has always been a bare platform, cleansed of every technical finesse."[35]

Bergman unquestionably endorsed this point of view (having often said much the same thing), but the practical result to which the idea led him in *Erik XIV* was manifestly different than that seen in the Sjöberg–Mörner performance. In Per Falk's scenography in Malmö, a single massive vault spanned the entire width of the stage, and this fixed arch, combined with Falk's etching-like projections on the cyclorama, communicated succinctly the drama's predominant mood of impending doom. Essentially, no solid physical apparatus at all was allowed to divert attention from the study of what Strindberg calls the "characterless character" of this moody and unstable Vasa monarch. Bergman's mise-en-scène eliminated the succession of localities envisioned by Strindberg altogether. Instead, large portions of the play were acted on the open, spacious forestage, where the magnificently costumed historical characters appeared against a simple background, like "a multicoloured gallery of Breughel-like figures" (*Sydsvenska Dagbladet Snällposten*). The undivided emphasis of this performance was thus on swiftly changing compositions of colourful human figures surrounding a focal point, the distinctly antiheroic, acutely analytical closeup of Erik created by Toivo Pawlo. The intensity of his characterization built steadily toward the moment of his abject humiliation, when his boycotted wedding banquet turns into a nightmarish orgy of rabble. In Bergman's hands this scene – which provided an interesting foretaste of the surrealism of the Goldmaker's Banquet in his production of *To Damascus* – became a veritable danse macabre, led by a ghostlike band of black and plaster-white human marionettes whose ghastly figures supplied a mocking contrast to the splendid attire of the bewildered royal couple. Spectacular this production surely was at moments such as this – but it was, at the same time, forcefully simple and direct in its quest for an uncluttered illumination of the inner spirit of Strindberg's work.

In this sense, these early Strindberg experiments at the Malmö City Theatre in the fifties form a direct and significant link to Bergman's revolutionary reinterpretation of *A Dream Play* at Dramaten in 1970. This being said, *The Dreamplay* (as Bergman called his deconstructed stage version) came as a totally unexpected occurrence that seemed, to critics and audiences alike, to mark a definitive distinction between then and now. Nearly all of the philosophical and mystical elements in the play were either omitted or transposed. In a performance in which stage settings as such played no part at all, the fifteen scenes into which this reconstituted but poetically faithful version was divided established a swiftly paced rhythm of juxtaposed images and contrasting moods, uninterrupted by the distraction of an intermission. "There are remarkably few extraneous elements in it, no convulsions, no exertion – all that seems to have been left behind," Leif Zern declared in *Dagens Nyheter* (March 15, 1970) following the premiere at Lilla scenen, Dramaten's 350-seat studio theatre. "In itself this represents an essential part of Bergman's method. He has produced an adaptation of the play that is in part quite radical, in part extremely cautious. But in both cases it is a matter of changes that find their basis in the text."

In its style and method, this new stage version represented a departure from virtually everything that had gone before, including Bergman's own attempt to adapt the play to television in 1963. The traditional identification of the Dreamer in all three of his voices (Officer, Lawyer, and Poet) with Strindberg himself was abandoned, as were all the elaborate visual effects and atmospheric back projections that had by then become fixed conventions of the Molander school. "No castle burns on the stage, no rhetoric flames in the dialogue," Bo Strömstedt wrote in *Expressen* (March 15). "Nor is it a biographical Strindberg Show in Molander fashion. Some wear masks in this production – but no one wears the mask of Strindberg." Within the stark and utterly simple physical framework devised for the production, no attempt whatsoever was made to reproduce, in literal terms, the multiple localities and spectacular stage effects called for in the stage directions. Instead, as Åke Perlström observed in *Göteborgs-Posten* (March 15), "the only thing we see – and hear – are the actors, who create the illusion that all these places are there on the stage. It is a brilliantly executed activation of the audience that we experience." The end result of this dematerialized, actor-oriented approach was, as Per Erik Wahlund remarked in *Kvällsposten* (March 15), to give the text a primacy "it seldom can acquire in more monumental productions; anyone who truly wants to listen to what is being said in the play has a unique opportunity here."

While Molander used a moderate amount of doubling for purely practical purposes, this procedure became an essential thematic dimension of Bergman's performance. A closely knit ensemble of twenty-four actors, who had been in rehearsal for more than three months, played the forty-three different characters identified in this version. All but nine principal performers took on two or, in a few cases, even three roles apiece. As the performance began, the entire acting company – including five extras and even the prompter – were summoned to the grey-black, curtainless stage, which stood furnished with a scattering of plain wooden chairs, some rough screens, and a single table. One by one, the actors emerged in twin streams from two circular (under normal circumstances backstage) staircases located at either side of the playing area. Moving to lively waltz music from a barrel organ, they flooded the stage in a carefully arranged but apparently random

pattern. A few busied themselves rearranging bits of scenery. Meanwhile, the Poet moved to the table at the centre of the stage, where he
drew up a chair and seated himself with his back to the audience. Then,
once the prompter and the black-masked Quarantine Master (among
the last to emerge) reached their positions, the entire company joined
to form a ring. Slowly the characters circled before the gaze (in the
consciousness?) of the Poet seated at his desk. "A metaphysical picture
of mankind's shadowy wandering in the wilderness" was how *Svenska
Dagbladet* (March 15) was inclined to see this evocative but wholly unspecific theatrical image.

    After fifteen seconds, in the midst of a step, the rotating circle of dream
figures suddenly froze in position. Quietly, the Poet read to them the six
simple lines of verse that were to set the tone for all that followed in this
performance:

> The earth is not clean.
> Life is not good.
> Men are not evil.
> Nor are they good.
> They live as they can,
> One day at a time.[36]

The reading of these lines – which belong in the original to Indra's
Daughter in the second of the scenes in Fingal's Cave – caused the
magical circle to dissolve. Some of the figures disappeared once more
down the circular staircases, but the majority simply took seats all around
the periphery of the action. Seated there they became both characters
waiting to be called into being by their creator and actors awaiting their
entrances. Agnes, the earthly counterpart of Indra's Daughter, and the
Glazier sat silently in a corner, eating. In a whisper, like a prompter
feeding an actor his cue, the Poet spoke again – "Agnes, the castle is still
rising from the earth" – and only then did the characters in the opening
scene acquire speech and dramatic life, as Agnes, looking about her,
began to discuss the Growing Castle and the prisoner who waits there
for his release.

    This opening scene deftly established the governing metaphor of
overt theatricality in this performance. From beginning to end, *The
Dreamplay* was anchored firmly in a world of theatre that became, in
turn, a *theatrum mundi*, a poetic and deeply ironic image of the world we
live in. In Molander's productions of *A Dream Play*, as we have seen, characters stepped out of the action from time to time to become spectators

20 In *The Dreamplay*, the starkly dematerialized version created by Bergman in 1970, the Officer (Holger Löwenadler) tells Agnes (Malin Ek) and the Stage-Door Keeper (Birgitta Valberg, seated) about his Victoria.

(dreamers) of it. In Bergman's adaptation, however, this was not an occasional occurrence but a permanent dimension of the action, in which the onlookers on the sidelines retained a highly charged doubleness as actors in a performance and characters waiting to rejoin their play.

The austere and eminently flexible stage setting designed by Lennart Mörk was, in effect, hardly a stage setting at all. The playing area was opened to the full width of the building, and the bare firewalls and overhead rows of projectors were as fully exposed to view as the players themselves. Any sense of separation between actor and spectator was obliterated completely by eliminating the dividing line of the proscenium arch and extending the floor of the stage out over the first rows of seats. The fixed point of focus and energy in the stage composition was clearly the simple table placed at the front of the stage, squarely in the middle of the proscenium opening. Around the Poet's table – beneath which he occasionally crept to eavesdrop on "his" characters – most of the scenes in the play were arranged. The theatre corridor, the cathedral where the degree ceremony is held, the Lawyer's suffocating chamber, even the enigmatic cloverleaf door itself were always represented in the simplest possible manner, by means of rudimentary, rehearsal-type screens that could easily be put in place and as easily removed. Sometimes only the Poet's table itself was needed, as was the case when he simply recited the second of the Fingal's Cave scenes to Agnes, stage directions and all. A small platform at the rear of the stage was its only elevation, and behind it the audience saw a large red, non-figurative design that contributed the one patch of colour in an otherwise grey-black world. (Mörk's tantalizing optical rebus led to a feverish guessing game among the critics, who professed to discover in it a picture of everything from "the burning castle of the dream" or "the human circulatory system" to "flickering flames from the earth's interior" or, in the case of one especially lively imagination, "the inside of the eyelid as we see it when we doze off, when we dream.")

The divine presence of an omniscient Indra and his Daughter, itself an afterthought on Strindberg's part, inevitably became a sublimely absurd poetic irrelevancy in this emphatically down-to-earth version of the play. Yet unlike Molander, who had eliminated this dimension entirely in his final production of *A Dream Play* five years before, Bergman chose instead to divide the composite character of Indra's Daughter into two distinct and independent roles. The utterly vulnerable Agnes, played by the young Malin Ek with poignant openness and clarity, was visibly and defenselessly human, stripped of the divine power to reascend from earth that renders the Daughter's suffering more equivocal in the original. By contrast, Kristina Adolphson's stately and dignified portrayal of the Daughter – the divine half of the equation – emphasized the aloofness of that shadowy deity. She and Indra (renamed the Scald here) remained, throughout the performance, remote presences from a rhapsodic, scaldic world of fantasy that existed perhaps solely in the Poet's lively imagination.

As for the problematic prologue in the clouds, Bergman did not eliminate it as Molander had finally done, but interjected it instead (slightly cut and rearranged) into the ongoing action, performed as a bit of theatre-in-the-theatre at the beginning of the first scene in the Theatre Corridor. "Yes, life is hard, but love conquers all. Come and see!" the Poet tells the bewildered Agnes at the end of the scene with the Officer's parents (taking the line that belongs to the Daughter at that point in the original). Then, as these two sat to one side, Indra and his Daughter rose from their chairs in the background and, in full view, mounted the raised platform-stage at the rear, to the accompaniment of polite applause from the other characters. Mörk's enigmatic red pattern glowed, and a gushy romantic adagio was played on an old piano. At the end of this recitation of the prologue, when Indra had completed his imperious brief of instruction to his Daughter ("Have courage, child, 'tis but a trial"), she sank to her knees ("I'm falling!"). A moment later, as the divinities left their platform and retired to seats in the background, a swirl of players again filled the stage, and the interrupted action resumed. The appearance of the Bill-Poster with his placards and his green fishing net, the Prompter carrying a piece of scenery, and the Stage-Door Keeper with her unfinished star coverlet and her heavy shawl of sorrows proclaimed the beginning of the Theatre Corridor scene. And here, the tragicomic spectacle of the Officer (Holger Löwenadler), waiting patiently for Victoria with his bouquet of withered roses, became a hieroglyph of human disappointment and self-deception that gave the lie to all the spurious metaphysical consolation of Indra's divine design. "The entire Indra phenomenon is transformed by Ingmar Bergman into the supreme theatrical gesture," wrote *Svenska Dagbladet*. "But perhaps Bergman feels that Indra's Daughter is no more than the dream of someone who knew that Indra never had a daughter, and that Agnes is in reality something quite different: the mortal woman, imperturbable in her endurance and her humanity."

As this remark suggests, Indra's Daughter seemed in this performance to be the Poet's dream. Her later appearances at the end of the play were again removed from the reality of the situation and seemed simply expressions of the Poet's creative imagination. Seated at his table for the second Fingal's Cave scene (entitled 'The Poet' in the production script), he began to read to Agnes the strophes on poetry, dream, and reality, and his reading in turn called forth, as it were, the presence of the Daughter and the Scald on the high platform at the back. Eventually the short recitation became a duet and even a trio when the Scald joined in, but no "soft music" accompanied it, no rolling billows were seen or heard, and no leisurely discussion of "life's unsolved riddle" was allowed to interrupt the insistent flow of the dream toward its conclusion.

In this respect and in others, the greatly expanded role of the Poet – played with effectively restrained intensity by Georg Årlin – replaced the figure of Indra's Daughter as the controlling consciousness in the work. His was the only character to be given a more important function than in Strindberg's text – where, of course, he appears quite late in the action. Here, he was present throughout but seemed more often to be a detached observer wandering through the proceedings, rather than a deeply engaged participant in them. At times, he appeared to listen to the conversation of the characters as if to a play that he himself might have written. And he, rather than the Officer, became Agnes' guide to the brief, dazzlingly white glimpse of the "paradise" of Fairhaven, which was abruptly juxtaposed in this production with the harsh realities of Ugly Edith's misery, the Schoolmaster's savagery, the pathetic plight of the Blind Man (played by Hans Strååt, who was also the Scald), and the drudgery of domestic duties that Agnes, deprived now of the comforting ability to "return to the place from which [she] came," seems unable to escape.

The highly ironic theatricalism of Bergman's production was epitomized in his rendering of the Degree Ceremony in the Cathedral, singled out by virtually every reviewer for its extraordinary pantomimic expressiveness. The grandiose formal trappings that had traditionally adorned this scene in Molander's day were firmly set aside, so that only a stark dream image of the sensation of human humiliation remained. The Chopin Funeral March, always Molander's favourite musical choice for the episode, was turned into a rowdy academic fanfare for the proceedings. The "cathedral" itself was indicated by the simplest of devices: a contorted tableau of human bodies was arranged upon the Poet's table to suggest an altar painting of the crucified Christ, arms outstretched and head bowed beneath a crown of thorns. Behind this crucifixion tableau, other shadowy figures crept forward with long, black screens – the pews of the church – from behind which they watched. The academic procession, too, had the distorted proportions of a dream. The standard-bearers of the four faculties were mini-scholars, played by children, wearing formal attire and student caps. A dignified gnome assisted the Chancellor in his duty of conferring laurel wreaths on the doctoral candidates. Entering this bizarre scene, the Lawyer (played by Allan Edwall and later in the run by Max von Sydow) found himself literally trapped in a nightmarishly logical Chaplinade from which he could not extricate himself. This "terribly ugly, unsuccessful, embittered character in an old tailcoat, shiny with use, that hangs around his shoulders" (Zern) stumbled onto the stage, bowed to the assembly, and he discovered that he was still wearing his galoshes. He tried desperately to unbuckle and remove them, only to be assaulted by the foul smell of his wretched old coat, heavy as all his clothes are with "the stink of other men's crimes." Quickly the sniffing spread; soon everyone present was holding his or her nose. In his mortification the Lawyer then tried to remove the offending garment – with the result that his trousers fell down, and he was reduced to the ultimate indignity of hopping about, unable to pull them up again. All the other characters were crowned with laurel; the

Schoolmaster even did an ecstatic war dance of joy. Only the humili-
ated advocate was turned away and obliged to rest content with a more
"appropriate" crown – the crown of thorns that Agnes took from the crucified Christ in the tableau and placed upon his head. One final ironic
pirouette punctuated the scene. After the crown of thorns had been cast
aside, the Poet strolled forward from the background, picked it up and
tried it on for size before a mirror (the audience), cocked it at a rakish
angle, like a *chapeau claque*, and strolled away.

The play concluded – in a scene Bergman entitled "Many People
become Visible" – in the same way it had begun, with the assembling of
the characters around the Poet's table. Each one brought forward his or
her emblem of sorrow to be burnt – the Stage-Door Keeper's shawl, the
Officer's roses, the Glazier's diamond, the Quarantine Master's black
mask (beneath which his own face turned out to be just as black), and
the rest. "Instead of casting their masks or their symbols into the fire,"
Wahlund wrote in *Kvällsposten*, "the figures stepped forward one by one
to the Poet's desk and laid them there. The play has ended, the vision has
vanished, and the characters who searched for their author can wander
back into the darkness." The Poet's concluding lines – spoken by Årlin
"with moving restraint, as a confidential message directed straight to the
audience" – were once again "borrowed" from the dialogue of Indra's
Daughter, who made her own farewell before he spoke:

> In the moment of goodbye,
> When one must be parted from a friend, a place,
> How suddenly great the loss of what one loved,
> Regret for what one shattered.[37]

"He steps forward to the middle of the stage, all the others gather around
him, as he contemplatively and quietly speaks of parting and of the
process of living," the Norwegian reviewer for *Dagbladet* (Oslo) observed.
"Because all ornamentation has been eliminated, the words, the actor's
voice, and the faces – so far forward on the stage that they appear as
closeups – succeed in engraving the Poet's vision upon each spectator's
imagination."

In its closing moments, however, the focus of this performance shifted
from the artist to his suffering creation. As the actors suddenly left the
stage, Agnes remained behind. The spotlight on the Poet's table was
extinguished. There was not even a hint of the symbolic visual images –
the burning castle (rarely flowering), the redemptive cross, the projection
of human faces on the cyclorama – with which productions in the past

had usually concluded. The intellectual function of this imagery was superseded by the simple emotional reality of the figure of Agnes, the woman who had taken upon herself all of mankind's suffering in her heavy grey shawl, now seated alone on the empty stage, her hand pressed convulsively to her face in speechless anxiety.

A DREAM PLAY IN THE CONTEMPORARY THEATRE

Like Molander's first production of it thirty-five years before, Bergman's reinterpretation of *A Dream Play* in 1970 unquestionably marked a critical turning point in the work's performance history. The elimination of conventional scenery completely and the distillation of the text into a tautly scored chamber-play format opened a new perspective on the play that fostered an upsurge of innovative and sometimes very unusual productions at smaller theatres both in Scandinavia and elsewhere. A good example of the Swedish experiments catalogued by Gunnar Ollén was the "neosimplified," heavily cut version staged by Lars Svenson at the Hälsingborg City Theatre in 1975, which reflected what Ollén calls "the tendency to perform even Strindberg's most visual drama on a virtually naked stage, with the actors' Grotowski-inspired 'body language,' their mime and physical expressiveness, as a surrogate."[38] Another kind of simplification was put in play at the tiny Traverse Theatre in Edinburgh when it opened the first professional production of *A Dream Play* seen in England (apart from a single Sunday evening performance in London more than forty years earlier) in 1975. Here the performance text was Michael Meyer's translation of the Bergman version itself, directed by Mike Ockrent on an open, multilevel stage surrounded by the audience on three sides. Inventive lighting effects and a rapid rhythm of cross-cutting helped to sustain the hallucinatory mood created by the fact that the play was performed by an ensemble of only nine actors, three of whom represented different faces of the character of Agnes.

Mysticism and ritual prevailed when Susan Einhorn directed *A Dream Play* at The Open Space Theatre in New York City in 1981, in a production much closer in spirit to Artaud than to Bergman. Einhorn's mise-en-scène stressed, by her own account, the play's concern with Buddhism, Chinese alchemical doctrine, and "the male/female principle" at work in the relationship of Agnes to the three men (Officer, Lawyer, and Poet) "whose sufferings she comes to witness."[39] In addition to the four actors who played these principal roles, four others – two men and two women, sometimes masked – handled all the remaining characters. Although Ursula Balden's setting was uncluttered (two chairs and a table), it was by no means uncomplicated. The combination of a mirrored floor and a ceiling piece of a mirrored mandala (the mystical shape that shows a circle within a square) hanging above the stage created an eerie atmosphere of reflected and refracted images. This effect was accentuated both by the candlelight glow in which some scenes were performed and by the patterns of light that played at times on the reflecting surface of the stage. The colour values in the production corresponded to its underlying metaphysical thesis, black representing the body, red the spirit, and white the soul. Even the movements and positions of the actors were arranged to reflect "the play's primitive symmetry": "Indra's daughter descends from the sky (circle), enters the earthly plane (square), interacts with a triangle of men, and returns to the sky (circle) again."[40] These geometrical signifiers were given added weight, in Einhorn's opinion, by stopping the action at certain crucial moments to allow the Poet, the Lawyer, the Officer, and Agnes to stand gazing at one another from their respective positions in the given configuration.

One of these moments occurred during the opening ritual of the Daughter's "incarnation" as a mortal woman, a ceremony no less fantastical in its way than Irene Triesch's descent in a golden mandorla (not to be confused with a mandala) sixty-five years earlier. The first appearance of this Agnes (Susan Stephens) was as a breathing form beneath a blanket made of silver thread ("meant to portray her soul looking for and finding a body for her journey to earth"). When the goddess appeared in her full regalia, she was surrounded by her triangle of men, who helped her prepare her earthly disguise by removing her ceremonial gown and crown and giving her shoes. The first human sound made by this Daughter of Indra was the giggling of a little girl that signified her "birth" as Agnes. And laughter continued to resound as a recurrent leit-motif in a production that attempted to re-emphasize not only Strindberg's preoccupation with religious mysticism but also his sense of humour.

In an interview with the authors in 1980, when he was planning an unrealized production of *A Dream Play* with Liv Ullmann as Indra's Daughter, Bergman used an interesting anecdote to describe the "sentimental" and "overaesthetical" elements he had previously felt obliged to eliminate in his 1970 adaptation of the play:

Strindberg had a corner in his home and there he had three palm trees – and in these palms coloured bulbs were hung. He had an armchair in this corner, and when his sister visited him and played Beethoven for him, he would sit there and flick on these coloured bulbs. Sometimes I get the feeling in *A Dream Play* that we are very close to that corner. And yet you must find a means of approaching it, you know, because that way of enjoying beauty is also wonderful. That sentimental, not very tasteful way. I think that my *Dream-play* in Stockholm was very pure and, in a way, very dogmatic. A little too pure, I find.[41]

After an intervening production of the play at the Residenztheater in Munich in 1977, in which he felt that the sheer monumentality and solidity of the stage setting had defeated his purpose, Bergman decided to return to the intimate and rather primitive surroundings of Dramaten's Lilla scenen for a new, much less radically edited revival of *A Dream Play* in 1986. His conception of it as thematically structured "chamber music" was firmer than ever, but this time he was determined to reincorporate the more rhapsodic passages and "overaesthetical" flourishes he had cut or parodied in 1970. While still using only a bare minimum of actual scenery, this greatly expanded revival revealed the inner landscape of the play as a fluid, densely layered montage of restlessly shifting images and impressions. It seemed, to the critic for *Sydsvenska Dagbladet* (April 26, 1986), "literally scored in musical terms," developing "from a single note on a piano into progressively richer harmonies" that spanned a wide register from the poignant and the tragic to the grotesque and even the absurd.

In a graphic but unobtrusive way, the performance again stressed the dimension of conscious enactment, of theatre-in-the-theatre. "By emphasizing everything in the play that is 'theatrical,'" Jens Kistrup observed in *Berlingske Tidende* (April 26), "he allows its vision of human reality and the human condition to emerge with even greater clarity." The intense intimacy of the actor–audience relationship that had characterized the earlier version was thus maintained at its full strength. Unlike his earlier *Dreamplay*, however, Bergman's new approach was specifically intended to integrate the work's complicated visual syntax more clearly and directly into his overall concept. "I wanted the audience to experience the back-alley smell of the Lawyer's office, the cold beauty of the snowy summerland of Fairhaven, the sulphurous shimmer and glimpses of hell in Foulstrand, the profusion of flowers surrounding the Growing Castle, the old theatre behind the Theatre Corridor," he remarks in the autobiographical *Laterna Magica*.[42] In practice this kaleidoscope of moods and impressions was evoked by a virtually cinematic progression of back projections, ranging from the luxurious colour of the Growing Castle's garden to increasingly bleaker nuances of black and white. The end result was a fluid, rapidly shifting stream of sensory images, flowing together to reinforce the emotional mood of a given scene and producing a sense of what one critic described as "the gliding, illogical simultaneity of reality and unreality" (*Göteborgs-Posten*).

Although the playing time of the new production (two and a quarter hours) added a full thirty minutes to that of the condensed 1970 version, one significant new deletion was introduced. Like Molander before him, Bergman now decided to eliminate the presence of Indra and his Daughter altogether. Instead, by introducing a few more cuts and transpositions than first anticipated, he made the figure of the Poet both the drama's controlling consciousness and also the intermediary between the actors and the audience. As played by Mathias Henrikson, he became the performance's co-director, so to speak, present from the very beginning in "Strindberg's corner" at the front of the stage. The area he occupied was a segment of turn-of-the-century *Jugendstil* reality defined by a clutter of objects (writing table, oil lamp, bookcase, stained-glass window, potted palm strung with coloured lights) that alluded unmistakably to Strindberg's own room in the Blue Tower. Opposite him, in the downstage left corner of the stage, Ugly Edith sat pounding out dissonant chords on an old piano, almost buried in a clutter of paraphernalia from the Poet's dream – a damaged crucifix, the figurehead of a ship, the cloverleaf door, a ticking clock, even the marble statue of a young girl (perhaps a greeting from Bergman's production of *The Ghost Sonata*). Between these two poles of poetry and music, the action of the Poet's drama unfolded in an open, magical area that reached to the back of the stage. To Lisbeth Larsson of *Expressen* (April 26), the play appeared as "his mise-en-scène, his poem, his dream, fragments from his life that materialize on the inner stage stretching into the deep-blue space behind him." In this sense the Poet seemed both the captor and the observer of his dreamed existence. Sometimes he sat listening or bending over his manuscript. At other times, he intervened directly in his mise-en-scène, moving a bit of scenery, directing Agnes, or comforting her by stroking her hair or drying her tears.

For, in this context, the Daughter (as she was still called in the production script) was above all the child of the Poet's creative fantasy, rather than the offspring of some remote Eastern deity. Bergman's most decisive move in the new version was to divide Agnes' role into three distinct voices and ages. In the opening scene (called Awakening: the Growing Castle), it was as a child that she conjured up for the Poet, through the strength of her unspoiled imagination, the unseen vision of a flowering

21 The emphasis on wide-angle figure compositions in Bergman's 1986 revival of *A Dream Play* is illustrated in this image of the Foulstrand scene. The Poet's corner occupies the left side of the picture. At the far right stands the Daughter (Lena Olin), like a spectator of a play-within-a-play, while the Poet (Mathias Henrikson, centre) and the other characters watch the bewilderment of the quarantined young couple, He and She.

castle that grows out of the earth. In the play that was the Poet's dream of life – his and hers – it was simply as a human being that the adult Agnes (played in these scenes by Lena Olin) was taught life's suffering and bitter adversities, without the luxury of a goddess' ultimate invulnerability. Instead, the very notion of divine creation – "human existence under the fumbling supervision of a distracted God," as Bergman puts it in *Laterna Magica* – was seen, in the second Fingal's Cave episode, as no more than the subject for an ironic performance within the performance. It was eagerly stage-managed by the Poet and declaimed by him and his protégé to "soft music" from an old Victrola while they posed before a photographer's screen depicting Böcklin's *Toten-Insel* (yet another nod to *The Ghost Sonata*).

At the moment in the play when the Daughter's earthly tribulations reach their climax, as the Lawyer returns for the last time to berate her for neglecting her "duty," a remarkable transformation took place in the Bergman performance:

LAWYER Your child suffers neglect. Do you want a human being to suffer on your account?
DAUGHTER Now my spirit is filled with discord. It has been broken and torn in two.
LAWYER One of life's small conflicts, that's all.
DAUGHTER O, how it tears me!
(*She collapses; when she arises, she is an old woman*)[43]

Without fuss or gimmickry, another actress replaced Olin. In the twelfth and final scene of this version (also called Awakening: Outside the Flowering Castle), it was an older, wiser Agnes, played by Birgitta Valberg, around whom the forty other members of the cast assembled. Weary and resigned now, she took leave of life and of her Poet, whom she in turn comforted as her own child, cradling his head in her lap as she explained life's riddle to him. Within a circle of fire suggested by six lighted candles arranged on the stage floor, she placed her shoes and the other characters in turn laid their various emblems of human suffering – the shawl of sorrows, the roses of withered hope, and all the rest. After the three Agneses and the others had disappeared into the darkness, the Poet remained behind. His play had vanished; his waking dream had come to an end. In this production, the final image was simply this last glimpse of the artist–dreamer, seated alone in "Strindberg's corner" in front of the stained-glass window. That single, evocative image could, in turn, be said to hold the essence of this director's approach to Strindberg – an approach that has invariably been grounded in a perception that the dreamlike quality of reality in the post-Inferno plays is always inseparable from the insistent reality of the dream.

From Bernauer to Bergman, the major productions of *A Dream Play* seen in the twentieth century have demonstrated a continuous redefinition of reality in the theatre, of what is meant by the illusion of "place" in theatrical representation. The pictorialism of Roller's designs and even the hybrid surrealism of Molander's early performances have eventually given way, in the latter's final mise-en-scène and in Bergman's work, to a simpler conception of the stage as an empty space in which the actors can and must themselves create the illusion of a castle or a stage-door alley or a cathedral. In the closing years of the millennium, however, both Robert Lepage and Robert Wilson came forward with new, highly individualistic performances of this work that relied chiefly for their effect on the use of elaborate visual imagery and spectacle. Neo-expressionism is perhaps the term that best describes the colourful mechanical wizardry achieved by Lepage in the Swedish-language production of *A Dream Play* that he created at Dramaten in 1994. Four years later, when Wilson was invited to the Stockholm City Theatre to stage his own panoramic version of the play, the imagistic style for which he is famous provided a voluptuous backdrop for a ritualistic meditation on Strindberg's text. "No other play in world literature," Evert Sprinchorn suggests, "contains so many pictures and images, scenes and characters that are quickly and lastingly imprinted on the mind."[44] It was precisely this atmosphere of rapidly shifting sensory impressions that the postmodern experiments of Lepage and Wilson sought to enact in terms of movement, changes of lighting, projected images, and sound.

The focus of Lepage's production in Målarsalen, Dramaten's intimate and flexible studio space, was the formidable feat of theatre engineering upon which his entire concept depended. He confined virtually the entire action of *A Dream Play* to a claustrophobic, three-sided cube suspended above water. As his expressionistic cube-universe turned, tilted, and spun on its hydraulic axis, lighting changes and richly decorative projections designated the shifting scenes and moods in the performance. "It creates a world that is both real and illusory at the same time," Michael Billington wrote in *The Guardian* (May 27, 1995) when the Swedish production was shown at the Glasgow Tramway. "[The cube is] an image of our boxed-in existence and yet a gravity-defying space where chairs appear to hang upside down and where ... characters emerge horizontally through slit-like apertures." "The actors move around this shifting space never able

22 A neo-expressionist glimpse of the Theatre Corridor scene, from Robert Lepage's production of *A Dream Play* at Dramaten in 1994. The theatre folk have emerged from the open trap in the floor of the cube, while the Policeman leaning over its top edge has come to prevent the opening of the cloverleaf door (the small panel at the lower centre of the picture).

to settle on solid ground," David Grieg added in *The Observer* (May 28) on the same occasion. "They perform wedged into corners or balancing precariously on the sloping floor, their very physical difficulties forcing a powerful dynamism into the language."

In all, only fifteen actors played the forty-three characters that appeared in Lepage's three-hour performance. Transformation, surprise, and inversion were his ruling metaphors, and nothing in his rotating cubist universe remained constant for long. A window became a trapdoor in the floor; the floor became a wall, the wall a ceiling. Often there was no ceiling, and characters peered over the top of the high walls at the action beneath them. After making her way down through green-black darkness into the "third world" of earth (where, as Indra reminds her, "its people dance dizzily/On the borderline between folly and insanity"), the Daughter (Francesca Quartey) awakened on the floor of what looked and sounded like a stable stall (a quotation, perhaps, of the Horse Guard Barracks) where she looked out through a small, brightly lighted aperture at the Growing Castle. The box turned, and she suddenly found herself yet deeper within this dungeon-world, where a child in an officer's uniform waited to be freed. Three actors appeared as different aspects of the Officer – as a young boy, a young man, and an older man (played by Måns Westfelt, who first appeared as the Officer's father). Eventually, all three were brought together to sit at the same desk during the Schoolmaster's withering arithmetic lesson.

Lepage's spinning cube gave a whole new meaning to the idea of scene changes. After the Daughter's very graphic seduction of the Lawyer (Björn Granath) following the humiliating Degree Ceremony, she was instantly transported into a nightmarishly skewed domestic hell where she found herself prostrate on the tilting floor beside the dreadful Kristin, clutching an infant. The variety of twists and turns in this experiential collage was not inexhaustible, however, and as it neared its end, its inversion of traditional moments became more forced. The gathering of the Deans and the Right-Thinking People before the cloverleaf door became a rowdy parody of a press conference or a political rally. Instead of the customary défilé in the final scene, the theatre folk appeared in a trapdoor in the wall, tossed their sacrificial objects down into the pit of fire that had opened beneath the floor of the cube, and then slammed the trap shut again. After the Daughter wished Gerhard Hoberstorfer's enthusiastic but naive Poet farewell, he quietly descended into the flames below, to be followed shortly by the goddess herself. In the ensuing darkness, the sounds of chaos and dripping water were supplanted by a final shimmering vision of a huge water-lily floating in the ether.

The logic that linked this last decorative signifier to the preceding actions seemed tenuous. Indeed, much in Lepage's spectacular cascade of images appeared somewhat arbitrary, dictated by a purely intuitive logic that had its basis in the geometrical configurations of his ingenious but ultimately reductive concept. Within the confines of this concept, text and acting seemed to matter much less than the visual impression created. "Technology impedes the actors, who are obliged to adjust their energy to the gyrations of the cube," Leif Zern remarked in *Dagens Nyheter*

(November 14, 1994). "They are herded together in what finally becomes a ridiculous fashion on this minimalist playing surface, and in the midst of this advanced mise-en-scène the acting itself often becomes surprisingly conventional." Lepage's belief that "the future of theatrical art will depend on ancillary art forms" has, Zern continued, little to offer "those who dream of a theatre that springs from the encounter between actor and text."

The foremost contemporary exponent of the amalgamation of theatre with the other visual and performing arts is undoubtedly Robert Wilson, the doyen of American experimental theatre. Wilson's staging of *A Dream Play* in Stockholm in 1998 has subsequently been taken on tour in the new century to both New York and London; at the same time, an illustrated scene-by-scene synopsis of the production was posted on the Wilson Studio website, giving unwary browsers the impression that this represented an accurate summary of what Strindberg wrote. For, although Wilson has called his strange transfiguration "a new interpretation of August Strindberg's masterpiece," it was in fact not an interpretation at all but rather a non-interpretative "installation" (a Wilsonian word) that paraphrased, contemplated, deconstructed, and often even mocked *A Dream Play*.

Thus, in the scene he calls "ceremony in which the lawyer is refused graduation," four academics dressed in formal riding attire enacted an absurd mechanical dance before three life-size stuffed cows. During the Theatre Corridor ("opera stage door") scenes, the most conspicuous figure was a stuffed white stallion (a Jungian symbol of sexuality, one reviewer presumed to suggest). A highly exoticized Daughter of Indra (Jessica Liedberg) moved through her adventures on earth with the glacial control of a slow-motion gymnast. The Growing Castle that she entered at the beginning and the end was, in this case, an old, dream-grey frame house with porch and shutters that was (like the play) undergoing extensive interior renovation. "Robert Wilson has created a cathedral out of *A Dream Play*," Lars Ring wrote in *Svenska Dagbladet* (November 15, 1998). "Out of Strindberg he makes a world of his own, drawn from the turn of the [previous] century and the American east coast . . . Obvious interpretations do not exist here; the audience must understand or proceed on its own intuition. Of course, those who wish can argue that this is not Strindberg and that the concept is too obscure. And those who think they will discover new levels, new intellectual challenges will be disappointed. Wilson builds architecture from the text, a structure of spaciousness and time."

23 As Agnes (Jessica Liedberg, right) takes her leave, the other characters in the play gather outside the grey frame house that was the Burning Castle in Robert Wilson's "installation" of *A Dream Play* (Stockholm City Theatre, 1998).

The Stockholm critics were clearly familiar with the rhetoric of Wilson's anti-intellectual aesthetic, and its vocabulary figured prominently in their reviews of his *Dream Play* montage. "Grand, warm, grey, and mild – and by no means without humour" is how Margareta Sörenson characterized the performance in *Expressen* (November 15). "Pictures one shall never forget are placed side by side. More dream than play, a theatre of picture and music where the strange feeling of dreams is for a brief moment given form." Others echoed, albeit obliquely, Leif Zern's earlier objection to the Lepage production, with its subjugation of the actor to the visual concept. "Robert Wilson's conductor's baton rules so firmly and decisively over the whole performance that one takes in its beauty with a kind of horror that it suddenly will shatter, that someone will end up sounding a wrong note that dispels the harmony," Claes Wahlin observed in *Aftonbladet* (November 15):

This is why it is also so difficult to say anything about the actors. They follow Wilson's instructions and appear to do it well. Carefulness and concentration in every movement create a strange suggestiveness – but it is not theirs. For even if the truth is to be found in body and space, it is still personal, in this case it is Wilson's truth – a truth that I gladly witness but cannot acknowledge myself compelled to share.

In general, Wilson treats production as a visual art from, in which words are always more or less secondary. Not least in the case of his Swedish-language production of *A Dream Play*, his performance conveyed the impression, as Lars Ring phrased it in *Svenska Dagbladet*, of "Strindberg as picture opera, as anti-modernistic mood painting." When seen by foreign audiences, meanwhile, the spoken text literally "disappeared" into the terse English surtitles that floated in the darkness above the stage. When Manhattan audiences encountered the experiment at the Brooklyn Academy of Music, it seemed to Bruce Weber of the *New York Times* (November 30, 2000) a "self-parody" reminiscent of "the Bergman spoof *De Duva* and Woody Allen's essay sending up drama criticism, *Lovborg's Women Considered*." Displaying "its characteristically stubborn indifference to the niceties of plot (he has invented wordless scenes of his own)," Wilson's approach seemed to this critic "both relentlessly beautiful and unyieldingly self-dramatizing, each of its tableaus reliant on a charged-with-feeling progression that is largely unmoored to language."

Wilson resists the temptation to synthesize as much as he resists interpretation. Accordingly, the individual components in his languorously

paced stream of moving images clashed and collided with one another
to produce the kind of fragmentation and disjuncture found in the work
of René Magritte, the early surrealist painter to whom he is sometimes
compared by critics. However, Michael Feingold's savagely funny review
in *The Village Voice* (December 6–12, 2000) was without any patience for
the studied incoherence of Wilson's Strindbergian installation: "It's all
about modeling, you see, people posed on ladders, or artistically raising
and lowering stylized pump handles . . . As a concession to Mr. A. S.'s
anguish, Wilson occasionally has one of the posed figures scream or
cackle for no reason, or interrupts Michael Galasso's graceful music
with an ear-splitting crash, but these things fade away so smoothly in the
general atmosphere of pointless gestures and lavender light."

The real comparison to be drawn in this case is to Artaud, whose own
production of *A Dream Play* seventy years before, while totally devoid
of the technical polish and sophistication available to Wilson in 1998,
made the same kind of deintellectualized effort to create "an interplay
of mental associations" that would appeal to "the deepest strata of the
mind." Artaud's commingling of "the false and the real," designed, as
he says, "to disrupt the senses' repose" as all true theatre must, finds a
close contemporary parallel in Wilson's complexly layered and colliding
images and figure compositions. Artaud's production failed, as we have
seen, because it contributed nothing to a fuller understanding of the work
at hand. Wilson's production made no effort to do so, asking instead to
be regarded as a work of art in its own right rather than an explication
of the underlying text. This line of argument seems to be taken more
seriously now than it was in Artaud's day. Wilson's followers are prepared
to watch a play differently, heeding his exhortation to "see the text and
hear the text and hear the pictures and see the pictures." He admits
being annoyed in the theatre when "what we see is always an illustration
or a decoration of what we hear." In his theatrical method, "what we
see is as important as what we hear – it should, and should not be there
just to serve the text."[45] Strindberg, the great revolutionary who laid
claim (not unjustly) to the invention of a new kind of play, in which form
is in itself the direct expression of its inner emotional meaning, might
well have found such an argument appealing – provided the pictures to
which the audience is asked to "listen" are manifestly *his* images. In the
case of this re-imagining of it, however, *A Dream Play* ("a stymieing thorn
for directors," as the man from *The Times* called it) served chiefly as a
springboard for Wilson's formidable theatrical virtuosity.

4

Chamber theatre: *The Ghost Sonata*

Among the darkest and most complex of the post-Inferno plays, *The Ghost Sonata* [*Spöksonaten*] is a dance of the dead that resonates with Strindberg's own deep personal anguish. "It has form and content: the Wisdom that comes with the years when our knowledge of life has accumulated and we have acquired the ability to comprehend it," he wrote to Emil Schering (March 27, 1907) upon completing it. "I have suffered as though in Kama Loka (Scheol) while writing it, and my hands have bled (literally)." Images of death are plainly uppermost in his mind here: Kama Loka, his subtitle for the play, is the Sanskrit term for the first stage entered by the soul after death, while Scheol is the Hebrew word for the realm where the dead lead a shadowy existence in a kind of trance or torpor.[1] While Max Reinhardt's interpretation of *A Dream Play* was criticized by some critics, notably in Sweden, as excessively macabre, his similarly dark and grotesque performance of *The Ghost Sonata* in 1916 seemed in perfect accord with the considerably more sombre atmosphere of Strindberg's last masterpiece.

This play represents another significant shift in style for Strindberg, as radical and experimental in its way as that which had occurred at the beginning of the post-Inferno period, eight years earlier. Described by him as the dramatic equivalent of chamber music, it became Opus III in the quartet of so-called chamber plays he composed for Intima teatern, the tiny experimental stage that he and August Falck operated in Stockholm for three intensely active seasons from 1907 to 1910. Falck, a young actor who was playing in a touring production of *Miss Julie*, came to Strindberg with a proposal to create an intimate theatre along the lines of Reinhardt's newly opened Kammerspiele in Berlin. The idea rekindled the playwright's life-long ambition to have a theatre of his own. It will, he boasted in a letter to the writer Adolf Paul (January 6, 1907), be "an intimate theatre for *Moderne Kunst*," for which he set out to complete a cluster of shorter plays written in the style he considered

suitable for the new chamber stage: "intimate in form, a restricted subject, treated in depth, few characters, large points of view, free imagination, but based on observation, experience, carefully studied; simple but
not too simple, no great apparatus, no superfluous minor roles." The
basic criteria comprising this definition of the chamber-play form – the
distillation of a single, unifying theme, its muted, unhistrionic expression
in compressed and fluid form, and the suppression of all distracting effects and disturbingly ostentatious backgrounds – apply in broader terms
to Strindberg's overall conception of what the theatrical experience in
general should entail.

It is clear in retrospect that Intima teatern sorely lacked the facilities to
realize Strindberg's complex vision in a play such as *The Ghost Sonata*. Initial plans for the new playhouse had called for a small art theatre of some
400 to 500 seats – considerably larger, in fact, than Reinhardt's elegant
292-seat Kammerspiele. In the end, however, the structure acquired by
Falck on Norra Bantorget, not far from Strindberg's new lodgings in the
Blue Tower, imposed a much greater degree of intimacy than the partners had originally anticipated. The attractive auditorium, decorated
in soft greens and yellows, held just 161 spectators, who were seated in
close proximity to a minimalist stage measuring only six meters in width
and four meters in depth. Within this severely constricted space, twenty-
four of Strindberg's plays were nevertheless performed during the three
brief years of the little theatre's existence. Once the young company of
eleven actors eventually found their feet and evolved a suitably subdued,
unaffected style of delivery, they fared best in such works as *Miss Julie*,
Easter, and the post-Inferno history play *Queen Christina*. (The unadorned,
drapery-stage mise-en-scène for the latter work, performed only a few
weeks after *The Ghost Sonata*, became, as we have seen, a kind of model
for Strindberg of the kind of simplified, non-representational staging
he felt was needed for *A Dream Play*.) However, among the least popular
and least accessible of the Intima's offerings were the difficult and elusive
chamber plays, all four of which were attempted during the first months
of its inaugural 1907–08 season.

The greatest challenge to be faced by the new and inexperienced
company was, of course, *The Ghost Sonata* itself, on the surface a compactly
and "conventionally" structured work that presents none of the technical
difficulties of *To Damascus* or *A Dream Play*. Instead, it depends squarely on
the director's control of the most delicate nuances of mood, atmosphere,
and intimation – or what Ingmar Bergman once referred to as "these
suggestions that strike us, powerfully and disturbingly, far deeper than

reason and analysis."[2] Evidently as a kind of warning about the existence of this dimension, the play was furnished with the subtitle "A Fantasy" before its world premiere at Intima teatern on January 21, 1908. The proscenium of the little stage was even decorated with two free renderings of Arnold Böcklin's *Die Toten-Insel* (*The Island of the Dead*), the painting that is meant to materialize in the background when the Hyacinth Room vanishes at the end. The suggestive bonding of fantasy and reality in this work seems for the most part, however, to have eluded Falck and his young charges. As a result, their performance caused considerable critical confusion and consternation. "It is necessary to preserve a sense of the visionary in speech and action, without thereby losing all semblance of reality," Bo Bergman argued in *Dagens Nyheter* (January 22, 1908):

Most of what happened in the theatre last night pointed in the right direction, and when the atmosphere was hopelessly shattered – as it was at certain points in the last act – the blame cannot be laid on the actors alone. To discourse about food and servant problems in stylized, sepulchral tones, and to be interrupted all the time from the kitchen by the Evil One herself (wearing make-up fit for a student farce) is bound to end as utter parody.

This would, by the way, not be the last time that a critic was to complain about the intrusions of the sinister Cook into the long scene between the Student and the Young Lady in the final movement.

The Intima cast seems to have adopted the affected diction and exaggerated make-up to which Bergman and other critics objected in order to lend a "spooky," spuriously Maeterlinckian atmosphere to the proceedings. "Words were not spoken but aspirated laboriously, as if in terrifying visions, by actors painted chalk-white in order to look as emaciated as possible," Anna Branting wrote in *Stockholms Tidningen* (January 22). Especially grotesque were the automaton-like participants in the Ghost Supper, the ritual of exhumation and psychic murder that begins with Hummel's assaults on the false Colonel and his guests and ends with his own destruction. Reviewers likened the figures in this scene to "mannequins," "wooden puppets," or "caricatures of humanity."

In the role of Arkenholz, the visionary Student whose journey of discovery the play charts, Helge Wahlgren appeared ghastly pale, intoning his lines and moving with the stiff walk and wooden gestures of a sleepwalker (or perhaps, as later directors have sometimes portrayed him, the dreamer of this dream play). Some two weeks after the opening, Strindberg found a chance to praise Wahlgren's acting in the little courtroom drama, *The Bond*, after which the playwright's letter took the opportunity to offer some unusually blunt criticism of his interpretation of Arkenholz:

But in *The Ghost Sonata* you did not play my part: the dashing student, the new, skeptical young man, who "doesn't go on about eternal love." . . . You weren't affected, but something else, which I can't find the words for . . .

I don't know what I can teach you. But I urge you next time in *The Ghost Sonata*: speak to the girl, it is with thoughts and words that he enters her soul.

And stress the poisonous effect of the flowers, which drives him mad like his father, and motivates his eruption.

In the final scene try gently to recall her to life, or at least take her hand and see if she is dead![3]

In contrast, Strindberg's many letters to Anna Flygare suggest that he considered this promising young member of the Intima ensemble perhaps the foremost exponent of the restrained, quietly expressive, and musically sensitive playing style he so strongly advocated. In the role of the Young Lady in *The Ghost Sonata*, she impressed the Stockholm critics with her "soulful, delicate, visually interesting portrait" of "the ailing human hyacinth" (*Stockholms Dagblad*). But not even the appeal of Flygare's poetically effective performance could salvage the mismanaged final movement of the play, staged by Falck not in an inner Hyacinth Room but rather in the same conventional *Jugendstil* salon setting used for the second act. Attired in an elegant dress and with a fashionable coiffure, Flygare's Adèle sat "leaned back limply in one armchair, the Student in another, both of them making the play's dialogue into something almost obnoxiously spineless and languid," Vera von Kraemer protested in *Social-Demokraten* (January 22). Nor did any vision of Böcklin's *Toten-Insel* materialize to signify the longed-for release of death. Instead, a pair of doors opened at the back of the small stage to reveal an indeterminate "landscape with pines."

In general, Strindberg's letters to his actors show us more than just his views on a specific text or performance; they also reveal the special nature of his relationship as artistic adviser to the Intima ensemble. Although lengthy periods of rehearsal were not unknown in this theatre, the small acting company generally seems to have functioned without a director in the usual, formal sense, relying instead on mutual consultation and adjustment. But Falck, who played the Colonel in *The Ghost Sonata* and normally acted in most of these productions, soon came to recognize the need for a director's objective coordination and guidance, not least when it came to the extremely difficult chamber plays. At the end of their first season, he invited Strindberg to undertake this new responsibility. "Not that we wanted to introduce a new style or transform our whole idea, but ... I thought that a director would be a great help with regard to rhythm and adjustment," he writes with some understatement.[4] Strindberg agreed, but after attending a few rehearsals of the season's new productions, he reverted to his preferred medium of written advice in the form of letters and memoranda, secure in his belief that "the actors found their own way during rehearsals, adjusted themselves, with the help of the director, to each other's acting, and obtained good results ... without my help" (*LIT*, 143). This implicit faith in the collectivist method was rooted in his distrust of the director–autocrat who imposes a single point of view and thereby, in his words, "threshes the play to pieces" with his constant conceptual analysis. Neither excessive rehearsal nor directorial conceptualization must, he felt, be permitted to interfere with the actor's own imaginative responses to the role and even his freedom to improvise.

Always, as Bark observes, the more astute of the two partners in theatrical matters, Strindberg tried but failed to persuade Falck to attempt a revival of *The Ghost Sonata* on a neutral drapery stage – an experiment that might have yielded exceptionally interesting results.[5] Instead, it was not until 1916 that Reinhardt's production of the play at the Kammerspiele in Berlin finally succeeded in unlocking its theatrical potential. Paradoxically, despite the playwright's stated objections to the new domination of the all-powerful figure of the director, he apparently did not hesitate to try incessantly, through Schering and others, to place his plays with Max Reinhardt, the virtual embodiment of the modernist theatre's ideal of the supreme artist of the stage. Although Reinhardt did in fact accept *Storm Weather* [*Oväder*], Opus One of the chamber plays, as early as 1907, none of his productions of the post-Inferno plays actually reached the stage during Strindberg's lifetime. The first work in this cycle, *The Dance of Death*, was produced at the Deutsches Theater in Berlin a little more than four months after its author's death in 1912. The impressive Strindberg offensive launched by Reinhardt quickly gained momentum with successive presentations of all four of the chamber plays, *Storm Weather* (1913), *The Pelican* (1914), *The Ghost Sonata* (1916), and *The Burned House* [*Brända tomten*] (1920). Most of these productions were seen on tour in Scandinavia, but none made a profounder impression there than the startling *Gespenstersonate* that appeared, albeit briefly, in Stockholm and Gothenburg in 1917. As we know, by the twenties Molander and others had begun to raise strong objections to Reinhardt's "Germanic"

expressionism. But in 1917, with memories of the inauspicious first productions of *A Dream Play* and *The Ghost Sonata* a decade ago still fresh,
Swedish critics and directors alike greeted his new interpretation as
a revelation that, as Per Lindberg declared, "opened our eyes" to the
visionary, musical power of Strindberg's last dream plays.

In the hands of Reinhardt's polished ensemble, *The Ghost Sonata*
emerged as a grotesque "nightmare of marionettes," as critics called it.
The driving force behind it was Paul Wegener's astonishing transformation of Hummel from the crafty and embittered old man Strindberg
drew to an expressionistic portrait of pure, diabolical malevolence.
"With a withered and spongy countenance, with a petrifying gaze and
mouth, with a biting and even bone-snapping tone, [Wegener] was
once again the consummate Strindberg actor," Fritz Engel wrote in
Berliner Tageblatt (October 21, 1916) after the triumphant Kammerspiele
opening. Norbert Falk's equally enthusiastic review in *Berliner Zeitung am
Mittag* (October 21) stressed the archetypal dimension of this actor's remarkable performance: "The demon in his war-chariot, the old man on
his crutches, seemed in Wegener's weighty portrayal the incarnation of
the Evil One, the symbol of destruction." When the production came to
Stockholm at the close of the same season, this ghastly, terrifying Hummel
fascinated the Swedish critics as well. "With his shrunken, stony face and
crumpled posture as he sat there in his wheelchair banging his crutches
and croaking in a hoarse voice, he left an impression as chilling as the
barren coldness of a dead soul," Olof Rabenius observed in *Nya Dagligt
Allehanda* (May 4, 1917). At first almost inert, this macabre figure seemed
to expand to almost superhuman proportions as he worked his spell
on the Student. Slumped in his wheelchair, a note in Reinhardt's script
reads, Hummel seemed "lost in himself, old, small, bent, exhausted, at
times as motionless as a dead man, but then, the long arms stretching,
grasping, [he] straightens himself, extends himself to full length, and so
appears larger than life."[6]

The unearthly atmosphere of darkness and dread established by
Reinhardt in his staging and lighting of the first movement of *The Ghost
Sonata* became, as it were, the outward manifestation of the inner spiritual darkness at the core of Wegener's virtual demonization of Hummel.
Despite its clear contradiction of Strindberg's own description of a perfectly ordinary street scene on "a bright Sunday morning," this atmosphere of "strange, sinister, spectral life" seemed fully as compelling to the
Swedish critics as it had been to their Berlin colleagues. "One sat totally
absorbed, bewitched, seduced by this bizarre, fantastical vision that lay

midway between genius and madness," Daniel Fahlström maintained in *Stockholms Tidningen* (May 4). The focus of this "fantastical vision" was the house facade in front of which the first act takes place – seen by Strindberg simply as a corner view of "a modern city house" but reconstituted by Reinhardt and his collaborating designers, Gustav Knina and Ernst Stern, as a monstrous (*übergros*), overornamented, and oppressive structure, "ghostly in its massiveness, its luxury."[7] Enshrouded in hazy grey light, both the house and the figures around it acquired an unreal, hallucinatory quality. Even Strindberg's ordinary Sunday sounds – church bells, organ tones, a steamship bell in the harbour – acquired ominous connotations in this eerie atmosphere.

As Hummel sat waiting beside the poster column, almost unseen in the semidarkness, a piercing white light picked out the marble statue of the young woman seen through the open window behind him, while the figure of the Milkmaid was also illuminated by the glow from a small light concealed in the drinking fountain where she stood. Thus, the revenants of Hummel's two victims – then ghost of the drowned Milkmaid and the statue of the girl who has become the mentally and emotionally ravaged Mummy – were suggestively singled out and paired from the outset. Meanwhile, standing with folded arms in the open doorway, the motionless figure of the Dark Lady cast "a silhouette in the greenish light . . . like a picture by Munch from the 90s" (*Svenska Dagbladet*). The allusion to Edvard Munch is apt and calls to mind the similarly dark, menacing atmosphere created by this artist's famous stage designs for Reinhardt's production of *Ghosts*, with which he inaugurated the Kammerspiele in 1906. During the years that followed, however, German theatre was swept up in a veritable frenzy of expressionist experiments and extremes that made Munch's bold transfiguration of Ibsen seem hardly more than heightened realism. By contrast, Reinhardt's *Gespenstersonate* came on the height of the expressionist wave and was strongly influenced by it and by the attendant pessimism of the war years. His emphatic use of expressionistic lighting, sound effects, and movements contributed to the overall view of Strindberg's play as a suitably grim reminder that, as Siegfried Jacobsohn put it, "the world is a madhouse, a prison, and a graveyard" where "we all belong in one of the three."[8]

The controlling consciousness in Reinhardt's expressionistic vision of the play was Arkenholz, the Student who unwittingly enters Hummel's shadowy nether world. Viewing events through the eyes of this clairvoyant Sunday child, the promptbook notes, "the spectator begins in a sense to see everything with sharper, ever sharper clarity."[9] Reinhardt supported this concept with a succession of purely expressionistic lighting changes. When the Student (Paul Hartmann) appeared for the first time, accompanied by the sounds of organ music and a distant ferry bell, he brought with him, so to speak, a flood of bright, neutral light that dispelled the prevailing grey, shadowy atmosphere and established normal illumination on the stage. Conversely, when he left the stage lost in thought at the end of the act, the brightness disappeared with him, leaving behind a silent pantomime of spectral figures that continued to gesture and quarrel soundlessly as the darkness deepened and the distant bells and organ tones were heard once more. Not unlike Helge Wahlgren, his predecessor in the original Intima performance, Hartmann displayed the slow, intoned speech and dreamlike movements and gestures of a sleepwalker. He was "wonderful at portraying surprise," Emil Faktor observed in *Berliner Börsen-Courier.* According to the promptbook, Hartmann's very emphatic expressions of astonishment – following his first, idealized glimpse of the Young Lady, for instance, and his horrifying vision of the green-faced Dead Man in his winding-sheet – regularly included the gesture of passing his hand across his forehead or over his eyes "as in a dream." This dreamer's bewilderment reached its climax when, at the end of the first act, Hummel returned in triumph with his retinue of beggars. "Like spectral dream-figures," Reinhardt notes, they doffed their caps, mouthed shouts, and mimed applause, but no sound of cheering or clapping was heard.

With its corrosive atmosphere of hatred and reprisal, the middle movement of the *Sonata* was the focal point in Reinhardt's production, as it would invariably continue to be in nearly all later productions of the play. The ghastly, festering confines of the setting for the Ghost Supper – where (as Bengtsson, the valet, explains) the living dead "sound like a pack of rats in an attic" as they munch their biscuits and crackers in unison – were delineated in lush expressionistic detail in Gustav Knina's scenography. The round (or in this case oval) salon was a lavishly decadent interior furnished with velvet drapes, potted palms, family portraits, tasselled, deep-purple furniture, and "venomous, fungus-green wallpaper with a mushroom motif." Exacerbating the noxiousness of the colour scheme were the vermilion walls of the room at the side where the Colonel sat writing. A clearer, softer light emanated from the Hyacinth Room at the back, where the figure of the Young Lady could be seen. Eerie, unreal lighting prevailed on the stage itself, except for a brief moment of luminosity when the Student eventually entered and then passed on into the Young Lady's room. The shadowy light made Hummel's surprise attacks on this chamber of horrors appear doubly sinister and fantastic. During the conversation between the two servants in the opening scene, a direction in Reinhardt's script states that the Old Man "swings himself soundlessly into the room on his crutches (rubber tips). Now he appears enormous, massive, diabolically inflated and saturated with evil intentions, He swings himself silently past the two, eavesdropping."[10]

As the four participants in the fateful supper gathered with the intruder around an oval table in the middle of the stage, the figures seemed to Jacobsohn "strangely dead and ashen-grey, weighed down by solitude, desolation, inhumanity. The vividness of a ghastly waxworks museum was achieved."[11] "In this spook séance," the omnipresent Bo Bergman recorded in *Dagens Nyheter* following the Stockholm performance,

a creative imagination was at work that succeeded in amalgamating all the disparate elements – the frightening, the grotesque, the bewildering – into a strange nightmare of marionettes, departed from life and leading a shadow-life under some secret curse. It was as though something behind and beyond the human held the strings of all these puppets with their mechanical and stylized movements. Everything was bewitched, hissing and whispering, murdering with words and with a Strindbergian hatred that alone seems to have outlived life [in them] and to have crept with its bestial soul into their humanity.

Hummel's long verbal assault on the silent figures seated around the table was scored by Wegener as a tense, steady crescendo, paced by the ticking of a pendulum clock. The speech rose to a peak of white-hot fury in which the life-lies of the bogus Colonel, the aged Fiancée, and the self-styled Baron were laid in ruins. The only one with the strength and human feeling to respond to the accuser was the Mummy, the parrot-woman who is Strindberg's most strikingly surrealistic image of an *anomie* that breeds madness and death-in-life. Gertrud Eysoldt played the role with a poignant sense of humanity underlying the bird noises and movements she made when she first appeared, hopping out at Hummel from her dwelling place in the closet. As she rose to stop the ticking clock and put an end to the duplicity of this "stealer of souls," her voice was firm and strong, and no trace of her parrot persona remained. Reinhardt audiences both in Berlin and Stockholm would likely have appreciated this moment between these two actors as a little *reprise* of their mortal combat as Alice and Edgar in their widely admired performance of *The Dance of Death* four years earlier.

24 Artist's sketch of Paul Wegener as Hummel and Gertrud Eysoldt as the Mummy in
Reinhardt's 1916 production of *The Ghost Sonata*.

Hummel's end came swiftly. When the Mummy rang a bell to summon Bengtsson, Reinhardt let it be echoed by the churchbells outside. Helpless and crumpled in his chair, he alone saw the reappearance of the avenging figure of the Milkmaid in the doorway, her arms stretched above her head in a gesture of drowning. She vanished when Bengtsson, yet another avenger, came with the death screen and placed it before the closet where the Mummy had lived her wasted existence. The tone of her orders to the man who had stolen her life was gentle and even kind, and he stumbled to the closet and disappeared behind the death screen without protest. "The Mummy stands deep in sorrow, moved and bent before the screen. The others sit motionless, staring before them," Reinhardt writes. "The front of the stage grows darker and more shadowy. At the rear, where the young people are, there is still a clear evening light. The curtain falls slowly on the harp tones of the final scene [des Nachspiels]."[12]

This direction signals an unbroken continuity between the second and third scenes of the play, whereas in fact its final movement appears to take place (judging from the Student's statement to Adèle) several days later, following Hummel's funeral. In general, Reinhardt's performance made every effort to forge a convincing link between the perilously static and potentially anticlimactic last scene and his overall directorial image of the play as the journey of the dreamer (whether the Student or the spectator) from bewilderment and confusion to insight and deeper understanding. The effulgence seen in the background at the end of the preceding scene now filled the new setting – the Young Lady's mysterious hyacinth room – with a strange radiance. In the shadows at the back, the motionless figures of the Mummy and the Colonel could be seen still seated at the table in the adjoining round salon. Although brighter and less overtly threatening than the venue for the Ghost Supper, the atmosphere of this small inner room was no less unearthly. The long white curtains that swayed like ghostly presences, the Buddha flanked by lighted tapers that stood on the tiled stove, and the profusion of blooming flowers repeated in the pattern of the *Jugendstil* wallpaper all evoked the sense of a bizarre shrine or a tomb. If the ritual of the Ghost Supper gave the dreamer a glimpse of hell, then this new station was perhaps a Kama Loka, a dead middle world where the lifeless wait torpidly for Death's complete embrace. "Outside, evening is falling," Reinhardt writes. "Violet colouring in the sky. In the room, an indeterminate, clear light, as if emanating from the flowers" – as indeed it did, for he concealed lights in the potted hyacinths that were placed on the window ledge and elsewhere about the room.[13] The eerie illumination coming from the flowers, the glow of the burning candles, and the yellowish-violet light visible on the horizon combined to create an atmosphere of timelessness and airlessness in which the grotesque verbal pas de deux of the Student and the Young Lady seemed suspended.

The intrusions of the Cook were no laughing matter in this perfor-mance. A monstrous figure clad in red, she came crashing through a small, wallpapered door in the corner as another reminder of the op-pressed and victimized world to which Bengtsson, Johansson, and the Milkmaid also belong – a world determined to tear down the cor-rupt and decadent society to which the Student has so naively as-pired. She "filled the doorway, her voice roared through the house, proletarian hatred smouldered in her eyes, Tschandala threatened with her kitchen utensils," Stefan Grossmann wrote in *Vossische Zeitung* (October 21, 1916).[14] The Student's astonished reaction to her presence ("What a strange house. It's bewitched!") was accompanied in Hartmann's portrayal by a revealing combination of gestures: like someone dreaming, he passed his hand over his forehead and seemed drowsy; like someone drowning or suffocating, he put his hand to his chest and gasped for breath. More alarming yet was the reaction of the delicate, timid Adèle (Roma Bahn) who, once the vampire Cook had appeared on the scene, started to display the hunched posture and parrot intonations of her mother, the Mummy. Arkenholz watched this transformation with dreamlike consternation, turning to look at the Mummy herself as she sat in the shadows of the round salon.

After the Cook's disappearance, Reinhardt's notes describe an increasingly aggressive, even Hummel-like pattern of behaviour by the Student toward the Young Lady. As Bark's commentary on this production observes, however, Hartmann's actual interpretation of the role seems instead to have maintained what reviewers consistently describe as a gentle, lyrical, sympathetically youthful tone – further evidence, in fact, that the ideas laid out in a Reinhardt promptbook were often modified by him or by his actors in rehearsal.[15] At the core of Hartmann's portrayal of the Student was a suffocating sense of entrapment that grew steadily stronger as his recognition of humanity's evil became more acute and the Young Lady's inability to survive this harsh truth became ever more obvious. He pressed his forehead against the glass of the window and drummed his fingers on the windowsill when he told the "pretty story" about Hummel's funeral and its dubious participants. As his final anguished account of his disillusionment reached its climax ("There are poisons that blind and poisons that open the eyes"), he threw open the window violently. Gasping for air, he took a deep breath as the wind began to blow into the stifling chamber.

After Bengtsson had brought in the death screen and the Young Lady had gone behind it, Hartmann spoke the Student's final words of consolation quietly and gently – "moved, filled with compassion," as Reinhardt puts it. As the wind became stronger and more audible in the room, the harp began to play. The vivid transfiguration with which Reinhardt closed the play made no use of Böcklin's painting but instead transposed Strindberg's conciliatory vision of it into a different yet fully consonant key. Stars filled the sky beyond the open window, while an unearthly white light flooded the room itself. The moans and whimpers coming from behind the screen mingled with the dying sounds of the harp. In the closing moments of the scene, the distant churchbells and organ tones that had marked the beginning of the Student's journey were heard once more. This time they blended with the sounds of the harp and muffled kettledrums to become a muted funeral march that accompanied the final intoned words of Arkenholz's benediction. Darkness filled the stage; only the starry firmament remained visible as the sounds and music slowly faded away. Quite unlike his subsequent productions of *A Dream Play*, an atmosphere of symbolist transcendence and peace seems in the end to have displaced the jagged expressionism of the first two movements of Reinhardt's *Sonata*. When the production visited the Lorensberg Theatre in Gothenburg, one reviewer aptly described the ending as resonating with a harmony "in which earthly life with its dirt and its pain is submerged as the perspective of the brighter and purer vistas of the life of the spirit is revealed."[16]

It was, of course, its jagged – and exciting – expressionism for which this popular and inflammatory production would be remembered. Reinhardt's *Gespenstersonate* was, in fact, not the first revival of the play after its imperfect premiere at Intima teatern, for Otto Falckenberg had already staged a very effective production of it at the Munich Kammerspiele fully eighteen months earlier. But the Reinhardt version fired the modernist imagination with its consummate theatricality and emotional intensity – qualities that no one else (except perhaps Strindberg) had previously recognized in the chamber plays. Thus, when a revival of the production reached the Casino Theatre in Copenhagen in 1920, it made an indelible impression on the gifted Danish playwright Kjeld Abell – not as a definitive interpretation of Strindberg's play, but as a revelation of a new way of experiencing theatre in general. As Hummel, Wegener's "ice-cold voice cut through the fever-hot atmosphere that streamed forth from the house," Abell writes in his vivid retrospective of the event. "Suddenly all thought was cut short. I ceased to think. During the brief moments in which the catastrophe took place, there was only time to feel. I felt with my eyes, my ears, my whole being." Looking back on this induction into modernist theatre, he concludes: "For me, *The Ghost Sonata* was not an answer but a breath that filled the theatre's space and caused it to live, to live in a question, caused me to live in that question."[17]

FROM EXPERIMENT TO RENEWAL

It was not until Olof Molander's rather belated revival of *The Ghost Sonata* in 1942 that a new production of the play would effectively match the technical brilliance and challenge the conceptual vision of the long-running Reinhardt version. Apart from an interesting Reinhardt imitation directed by Gyda Christensen (who also played the Mummy) at the Central Theatre in Oslo in 1921, the only noteworthy new performance of this demanding text was the American premiere presented by the Provincetown Players at their tiny theatre on Macdougal Street in 1924. The experiment was intended to launch and identify a new phase in the Players' existence; hence, in this context Strindberg's play was chosen not in spite of but "because of its difficulties of form as well as of content" – difficulties that would only enhance "its possibilities for experimental production – indeed, its need for that."[18] Eugene O'Neill, whose widely reprinted tribute to Strindberg as "the precursor of all modernity in our present theatre" first appeared in the Provincetown program for the opening (January 3, 1924), was the driving force behind this bold attempt to introduce the post-Inferno works into the professional American theatre. With the kind of play he himself was trying to write at the time clearly in his mind, O'Neill used his little essay, "Strindberg and Our Theatre," to extol the style of the "behind-life plays" (his term) in which Strindberg established himself as "the greatest interpreter in the theatre of the characteristic spiritual conflicts which constitute the drama – and blood – of our lives. . . . All that is enduring in what we loosely call 'Expressionism' – all that is artistically valid and sound theatre – can be clearly traced back through Wedekind to Strindberg's *The Dream Play*, *There are Crimes and Crimes*, *The Spook Sonata* [as it was then called], etc."[19]

Not everyone agreed, it is true. The prominent modernist stage designer Robert Edmond Jones, who co-directed and co-designed the Provincetown production of *The Ghost Sonata*, regarded it as "a horrible play about horrible people," and he reputedly did his utmost to cut the text liberally and to hinder O'Neill's more bizarre suggestions, one of which had apparently been "to emphasize every Strindberg cliché with an offstage trumpet blare."[20] Yet despite internal differences and a predictably hostile reception by the New York press (which the republication of O'Neill's essay in the *New York Times* was designed to refute), this pioneering performance had an encouraging intellectual and artistic impact on regional and university theatre groups across the country. This was the first production of the play to experiment with the selective use of masks: characters such as the Milkmaid and the Dandy (the counterfeit Baron) wore full-face masks to suggest the doubleness of their identities. The scenography itself, designed for the exceedingly intimate Provincetown

25 Hummel (Stanley Howlett, standing) confronts the Colonel's guests in the round
     salon in the Provincetown Playhouse production of *The Spook Sonata*, 1924.

stage by Jones and Cleon Throckmorton, also took a highly innovative
approach to Strindberg's stage directions. A surviving production photo,
depicting Hummel's confrontation with the supper guests in the round
salon, shows a setting made up only of two simple side wings, a forestage
area one step down, and an open cyclorama at the back. Upstage centre,
displacing Strindberg's white tiled stove, the statue of the young Amelia
stood on a high, mausoleum-like pedestal. Contained within this sinister
monument was the cupboard where the Mummy had her refuge.

Especially in light of the many thematic and dramaturgical connec-
tions between *The Ghost Sonata* and the later absurdist drama of Beckett
and Ionesco, it seems rather surprising that the play failed to inspire
greater interest in the French experimental theatre. Ionesco, for example, speaks of his own plays as "the exteriorization of a physic dynamism,
a projection onto the stage of internal conflict, of the universe that lies
within."[21] In a planned mise-en-scène for *The Ghost Sonata* that Artaud
drew up in 1928, the same year in which he staged *A Dream Play*, he
discusses the *Sonata* in quite comparable (albeit distinctly Artaudian)
terms, as a work likewise projecting "a sensation of something which,
though not on the supernatural or nonhuman level, is to some degree

part of a certain inner reality." The real and the unreal intermingle in Strindberg's play, he writes, "as in the brain of a man falling asleep or suddenly awakening to find himself facing the wrong way."[22] Artaud's production plan was not realized in practice, however, and when *La Sonate des Spectres* finally reached Paris in 1933, on a crowded triple bill co-directed by Marcel Herrand (who played the Student) and Jean Marchat (who played Hummel), the event made little impression. Sixteen years later, the eminent Beckett director Roger Blin staged the play (and also acted the Student) on a tiny stage in the crumbling old theatre hall at the Gaieté-Montparnasse, where it shared a cruelly lengthy double bill with Büchner's *Woyzeck*. The outcome was unrewarding for Strindberg's reputation. Blin – who had acted with Artaud but knew nothing of his planned mise-en-scène for *The Ghost Sonata* – told an interviewer he "was drawn to the play through its social applicability – food and money."[23] Unfortunately, however, what came across to the small handful of spectators who attended each evening was, in the words of one Swedish observer, "an incredibly festive caricature of German–Russian theatre in the Berlin of the twenties."[24]

Unlike these rather haphazard attempts, the intelligent amateur production of *The Ghost Sonata* directed by the young Ingmar Bergman in Stockholm in 1941 marked the beginning of a continuous effort on his part to evolve a dynamic theatrical solution commensurate with the dramaturgical complexities of Strindberg's play. Staged in a ninety-nine seat chamber theatre in Medborgarhuset (Community House), this modest performance was in fact the first real revival of the play in Sweden since Reinhardt's touring production of it startled Stockholm twenty-four years before. Snapshots of the event convey no hint of Reinhardt, but bear instead a distinct resemblance to the old photos of the simple, rather cramped productions given at Intima teatern in Strindberg's day. Bergman's inspiration to use the limited space and resources of his children's theatre in Medborgarhuset for an adult performance of *The Ghost Sonata* was a bold one. "However, I recall how the fragile ensemble was lifted as though on a wave by the immensity of the drama . . . to be supported in our inadequacy and not dashed to pieces by it," he wrote in a program article for his later revival of the play in Malmö. A year later, Bergman's note continues, "came the great, totally shattering experience" – the first of Olof Molander's five major productions of the *Sonata*, presented on the main stage at Dramaten in the fall of 1942: "What I experienced that night in the theatre seemed to me absolute and unattainable. And it seems so still."

Many shared the young Bergman's enthusiasm. Molander's epoch-making production rekindled popular interest in *The Ghost Sonata*. Again animated by his life-long study of Strindberg's drama as encoded auto-biography, Molander transposed the scenic music Reinhardt had discovered in the play into a more familiar and far less strident key. Perhaps the most remarkable visual signifier of this new approach was the stage setting that he and Sven-Erik Skawonius devised for the opening scene – a detailed replication of Karlaplan 10, the red-brick building where Strindberg had lived when he wrote the play (and which remained a Stockholm landmark until its demolition in 1969). Herbert Grevenius described the effect as "a stage picture to remember. Pure colour photography, it might seem at first. But there is a slight overexposure that soon manifests itself in a dreamlike clarity of shading and contour. And then that Sunday silence in the piercing sunlight" (*Stockholms Tidningen*, October 17, 1942). This startlingly hyperrealistic stage picture "evoked in a totally masterful way this sense of the chilling clarity of a dream," Nils Beyer agreed in *Social Demokraten* (October 17). "The red-brick house facade was incomparable; in all its ingenious banality, it became one of the most wonderful sights ever seen in a theatre, in a strange way so real and yet so unreal – and as if living a life of its own, an odd, panoptical sort of life filled with the day's shifting light and sounds of hoof beats, church bells, and impending thunder."

The muted, simple everydayness so eloquently described in these accounts seemed, to many of these critics, a conclusive repudiation of the macabre tone and overtly nightmarish effects of Reinhardt's earlier mise-en-scène. Yet, while no obvious sense of evil or distorted grotesqueness was present in Molander's rendering, the sharpness of focus and precision of detail in his opening scene created an intensified reality that was virtually magical, in which everything might be possible. Magic realism is a term that is sometimes used to describe the work of certain modern painters who, by employing an exceedingly exact realistic technique, try to convince their viewers that extraordinary and dreamlike things are possible, simply by painting them as if they existed. "Painting reality with an edge – with a meaning" is how the American painter Andrew Wyeth once described his own style in an interview. "It's what is behind it that's important . . . It's fairly true, but it's certainly not accurate perspective." In very much this same manner, Molander exploited cool, camera-sharp surface fidelity to create a charged image of a stifling prison-world of the spirit, into which the Student is drawn on his dream-journey.

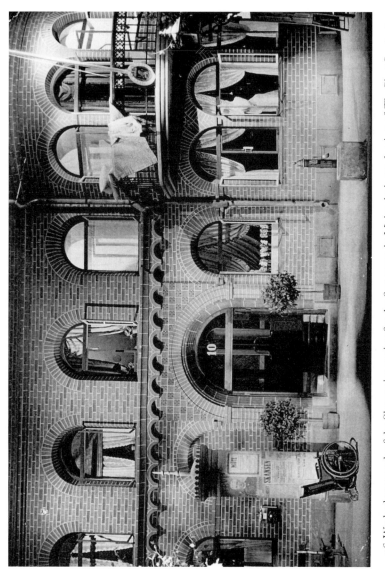

26 Work photograph of the Skawonius setting for the first scene in Molander's production of *The Ghost Sonata* at Dramaten in 1942.

Hence, there was no sense here of a "haunted" house or "spooky" inhabitants, as was the case in the Reinhardt model. Instead, Molander's production endeavoured throughout to capture the blurred, essentially non-existent distinction in the play between the living and the dead, that typically Strindbergian absence of any tangible demarcation between reality and dream. Dream infiltrated the realistic atmosphere from the very beginning, in the languid, virtually mesmeric prelude with which Molander brought his street scene to life. Standing silent and completely immobile in the doorway of the house, the black-clad figure of the Dark Lady seemed, to an observant viewer like Sten Selander, "to introduce a tone of unreality into the tangible ordinariness" (*Svenska Dagbladet*). In an article in *Bonniers litterera magasin*, Georg Svensson goes on to characterize the ominous presence of this black figure as "an omen of unreality, a discreet indicator that this clear light in which we see everything on stage is not the light of reality but that of dream and poetry."[25] Gradually the scene filled with ostensibly normal activity. The caretaker's wife polished the brass. Bedclothes were aired on the balcony. The Colonel strutted in front of his window. Shades rolled up, and people were seen moving inside the house and walking past on the sidewalk. "Then the ghostly atmosphere rises up out of the sunlight itself," as *Aftonbladet* put it. "The dead Milkmaid, who is the Old Man's guilty conscience, gives the Student a drink of water from the pump."

In Lars Hanson's remarkable reinterpretation of the role of Hummel, this character stood apart from the fantastical world about him. "In this strangely unreal reality, where people and apparitions move in the same marionette-like silence, Lars Hanson's Hummel emerges as the only one alive and active," Selander asserted. Paul Wegener's splendidly sinister and demonic portrayal of Hummel had set a precedent that would have been perilous to imitate, antithetical as it was to the more "familiar" style of acting and staging adopted by Molander. Hanson's performance took the character in a more psychotically complex and decidedly more human direction. With his exceptional facial expressiveness, he created a faceted figure who, while still the "ravager of human lives" that his servant Johansson describes, was also at times compassionate, wise, and even humanly vulnerable. "One should perhaps not say sympathetic," Nils Beyer observed, "but [he was] as kindly as this old man can possibly be played." Perhaps his most striking trait was what Beyer calls "a kind of philosophical mildness" that sprang from "the wise insight that human beings are not to be blamed, because it is life itself that has deformed them."

Hanson and his director laid the emotional groundwork for Hummel's final collapse by drawing attention to a crucial but overlooked moment in the second act when Hummel first gains access to the mysterious house. In Skawonius' design, the so-called round salon was depicted as a surrealistic pastiche of preposterous bourgeois pomp, floating on an immense floor rug in an empty black void. Tall windows, flowing drapes, and a bizarre, balloon-shaped chandelier suspended overhead all contributed to a sense of intimidating height. The marble statue stood in the midst of a shrine of potted palms, downstage right. A table and chairs for the supper guests were overshadowed by a towering, mock-baroque porcelain oven that also accommodated the mandatory ticking clock on a mantle. Here, as Selander remarked, Hummel "was helplessly lost in a world where nothing was impossible or unreasonable." Left alone for a few moments before the sudden emergence of the Mummy, Strindberg's stage direction notes that Hummel "*wanders about the room, fingering objects; adjusts his wig in front of the mirror; then turns again to the statue.*" The actor and the director took up this hint of nervous self-consciousness on Hummel's part and expanded it into a telling revelation of a deep-seated fear underlying his ruthless exterior.[26] "When he was left alone there, one saw in an instant the mighty Hummel exposed in all his pompous helplessness," Oscar Rydqvist noted with approval in *Dagens Nyheter*. This sense of inner anxiety and vulnerability – briefly reasserted visually in the threatening reappearance of the Milkmaid – was the factor that made this Hummel human. Yet at the same time it was also the sign of a fragmented, "characterless" self that was doomed to collapse, defenceless and speechless in the face of the Mummy's withering denunciation. "The old thief was transformed into a tragic figure," Beyer was inclined to assert, "and his wretched end was gripping as, broken and half-crippled, he dragged himself into the closet to take the Mummy's place."

This transformation of Hummel from malefactor to victim of his own malice coincided with and corresponded to the even more graphic physical and emotional transformation of Marisa Ekström's Mummy from a caricature of humanity into a rational and articulate human being. Ironically, it was Hummel himself who, as a debased and unwitting Pygmalion, turned the statue back into a living woman, forced by his evil schemes to rediscover and reassert her own lost humanity. "When she stopped the clock and held her speech of judgment over Hummel, it grew silent in Dramaten's auditorium as seldom before," Rydqvist commented. "Here was *Humanity* speaking in all its trembling nakedness."

With the leather-brown face of a mummy (or a thousand-year-old parrot, Beyer suggested), the gestures and demeanour of some outlandish bird, the squawk of a parrot, and a strange costume of ruffles, feathers, and layers of lace, Ekström presented a physical appearance that accentuated the abruptness of her change, making it seem all the more magical and symbolical. "She handled the metamorphosis from parrot to woman masterfully," Beyer remarked, "and she virtually took on a kind of grandeur in that final confrontation."

It was at this point in the production, Grevenius felt, that "symbolism takes over and acquires scope," displacing what he otherwise objected to as "its somewhat intrusive sense of realism." By rotating a turntable stage, Skawonius' set for the Colonel's oppressive surroundings faded into the shimmering brightness of the Hyacinth Room in a swift, dreamlike manner. The purely theatricalist style of the setting for this final movement struck a fundamentally different chord than the "magic realism" of the opening street scene. Skawonius created a liminal space composed of only two high walls, joined upstage centre at an acute angle, thereby forming a triangle whose base was the curtain line. Both the unusual geometry and the eerie radiance of "the testing room" (as the Young Lady calls it) conveyed a distinct air of unearthliness. The only access was through a curtained archway leading to the adjoining round salon, where the Colonel and the Mummy could be glimpsed sitting in silence. The furnishings of this strange chamber were sparse and by and large as Strindberg describes them in the text: a stove with a Buddha on it, a harp standing on a small oriental rug, the rickety writing table, and tiers and banks of potted hyacinths on either side. A curtained alcove with a bed gave the room a touch of boudoir that the playwright had not thought of.

In the more freely symbolic third act, the Student (Frank Sundström) and the Young Lady (Inga Tidblad) brought the music and poetry of Strindberg's dialogue to life with unusual force (in what was, after all, the first major professional production of *The Ghost Sonata* in Swedish since Strindberg's own day). "All of the play's poetry was ultimately distilled in the dialogue between them," Beyer observed. Uninterrupted by the actual appearance of the Cook, who in this instance remained a menacing silhouette seen through the translucent wall, their scene together became a long duet of love and despair, hope and disillusionment, life and death. Although Sundström's Arkenholz is described as being swept up in "steadily more overwrought moods," he took no active part in the destruction of the Young Lady, whose death was the result of her own

27 Work photograph of the setting for the Hyacinth Room in Molander's 1955 revival
of *The Ghost Sonata*. At the end, the two walls of the set turned on pivots and
disappeared from sight, leaving only the free-standing objects – the hyacinth clusters,
the writing table, the harp and stool, and the Buddha on a pedestal – visible against a
black background.

weakness and inability to bear the truth of the Student's bitter disappointment and (in the Shavian sense) heartbreak. Having overcome
ignorance and sensual longing, two of the three Poisons of which
Buddha speaks, Arkenholz seemed, in the mystical apotheosis with which
Molander replaced Strindberg's ending, about to triumph as well over
the third poison, desire for individual existence. As the harp sounded
again, the two walls of the triangular room parted and disappeared to
reveal an impenetrable darkness beyond, into which the Student walked
with head held high. Two work photographs for the 1955 revival at
Dramaten, for which the same mise-en-scène was used, clearly show the
striking visual effect achieved by the room's transfiguration.

Grevenius was among those critics most moved by the religious mysticism of a conclusion he saw as an affirmative expression of "the yearning of all humankind" for reconciliation and peace. "It is a hymn-like ending," he wrote. "Such as it is integrated here, even this troubled Strindberg work moves and liberates us." The transcendental character of this image was, as we have now seen, typical of Molander's Strindberg in general – and it is also the element in his work least compatible with later postmodernist approaches to the playwright and to this play in particular. For a radical young director like Staffan Valdemar Holm, whose New Scandinavian Experimental theatre presented what might be called an absurdist deconstruction of *The Ghost Sonata* in Copenhagen in 1989, the play was essentially "a dream of the absolute happiness that can only be fulfilled in that very cold orgasm we call death." For Molander, the post-Inferno plays were all very concrete expressions of their author's own inner psychic struggle for meaning in life. His strongest objection to Reinhardt's style was what he saw as its failure to grasp and come to terms with this ordinariness, with Strindberg's view of life and dream as essentially indistinguishable states. As such, his own productions strove to incorporate the razor-sharp fragments of ordinary (autobiographical) reality that are embedded in the playwright's vision. The most striking example of this is seen in the detailed replication of Karlaplan 10, Strindberg's own building, at the beginning of *The Ghost Sonata*, as the house within which the events of the play were by implication seen to take place. His biographical realism was, Grevenius noted cautiously, "not the only right solution, but it did make a clean break with the conjuring tricks that had long flourished as part of the Strindberg mystique."

Like Reinhardt's controversial "expressionism," however, Molander's method also provoked critical disagreement. When he restaged his version of *The Ghost Sonata* at the Royal Theatre in Copenhagen as part of the Danish national theatre's bicentennial in 1948, his psychobiographical interpretation of the text prompted the popular critic Frederik Schyberg to shrug off the darkness of the play's vision as mere personal idiosyncrasy, without relevance to the new postwar world. "The play shows us Strindberg's quarrelsome genius at the end of his days in a superfluity of his magical expressiveness," Schyberg declared in *Politiken* (February 18), adding that the work is also "a psychologically interesting manifestation" of the argumentative character of the artistic temperament in general. "But does the *content* of the play contain anything of concern to the contemporary individual?" he demanded, hastening to answer his own rhetorical question with italicized emphasis: "I think not: *it does not concern us.*" True, this otherwise intelligent critic's astonishing outburst relates to the play rather than to the performance, but one has the sense that his opinion of the former was shaped by the impression left by the latter. If nothing else, the comment serves as a reminder that this particular play has never ceased to be the bone of contention Strindberg knew it to be, especially when seen in performance. While Molander's influential reinterpretation of *The Ghost Sonata* is justly regarded as a turning point, a seminal reassertion of its performability, Ingmar Bergman's subsequent variations on Strindberg's chamber music have been of crucial importance in continuing to keep this play fresh and alive for contemporary audiences.

THE BERGMAN VARIATIONS

The essence of Ingmar Bergman's attitude to *The Ghost Sonata* and, by extension, to Strindberg as a whole is contained in a statement he made to the cast for his 1973 production of the play at the Royal Dramatic Theatre in Stockholm:

Everything in this production must be close to us, naked, simple. Simple costumes, hardly any makeup. The characters in the play are not monsters. They are human beings. And if some of them – the Cook, for instance – appear to be evil, it does not follow that they must look evil. The point is that they behave in an evil way toward the figures on the stage, and we must perceive the evil through the reactions of these figures. If we undervalue the audience's ability to take note of reactions, we corrupt the theatre.[27]

Clearly, the long shadow cast by Reinhardt's *Gespenstersonate* and the inherently evil Hummel of Paul Wegener had now vanished conclusively from the face of Strindberg's theatre. Writing about Bergman's earlier production of the *Sonata* at the Malmö City Theatre in 1954, critic Allan Bergstrand (*Arbetet*) made the observation that any director who attempts this play is in a sense faced with a basic choice: "whether to stage it, as Molander has done with all his Strindberg productions, in terms of naturalistic scenes into which mysticism and unreality are blended as completely natural elements – as they seem to be for all believers in spirits – or, instead, to opt for an undecorated expressionism in which characters appear out of or disappear into the darkness." Ollén, who quotes this remark in his study of Strindberg, adds that Bergman chose "by and large a middle road" – a kind of conflation of Reinhardt's unadorned expressionism and Molander's "fantastic realism," scored

in three distinct tempi that moved from the dream-sharp everyday details of the first act to a much more stylized milieu of heavy drapes in
the second act and, finally, to a starkly simplified, symbolic hyacinth
room in the final movement.[28] By the time of the 1973 revival, however,
the "middle road" had led Bergman far beyond the confines of either
conventional expressionism or the traditions of the Molander method,
to the adoption of his own highly expressive, actor-oriented style of
performance.

Bergman's first professional staging of *The Ghost Sonata* in 1954 was not
an outright repudiation of the Molander tradition of the forties (which
he eulogized in the program), nor was it in any sense an imitation of
it. "Ingmar Bergman acknowledges his debt to Molander, but this new
mise-en-scène possesses his own personal strength, his intensity, and a
discipline that is impressive," the Danish critic Svend Kragh-Jacobsen
declared in *Berlingske Tidende* (March 7, 1954), in an interesting review that
draws direct comparisons with the Molander production in Copenhagen
six years earlier. Bergman's special ability to stimulate his actors to a
forceful and physically emphatic expression of scenic emotion found an
ideal field of play in the middle movement of the play, which Kragh-
Jacobsen describes as shaped by "an imagination that at the same time
subjugates the stage space and fills it, inspires the actors and drives them
to the uttermost limits." In this scene of exhumation and psychic murder,
Bergman's interpretation translated all that is purely verbal in Strindberg
into fiercely concrete physical articulation.

Benkt-Åke Benktsson was a voluminous Hummel – "a colossus on light
feet, a perverted Prospero, an evil God the Father," Ivar Harrie called
him in *Expressen* – whose character was delineated in terms of sharply
etched emotional (not psychological) peripeties. His muted, scheming
tone in the first act gave way to the overpowering cynical force with
which he laid bare the hypocrisy and mendacity of the Colonel and his
household, only to be displaced in turn by helplessness and terror as
he found himself unmasked in turn and destroyed the woman who was
once his young love Amelia. "His powers were first unleashed in the second act," Kragh-Jacobsen remarked. "The frightening, almost magical
gleam that is suggested in his glance catches fire. His voice turns to thunder." Once he had systematically stripped the Colonel – Georg Årlin's
"marionette on wooden parade" – of his property, his rank, and even the
dignity of his title as father, the vampire himself fell victim to the vengeful
fury of Naima Wifstrand's Mummy. No grotesque parrot-woman now,
Wifstrand became the avenging dead who remorselessly settled accounts

with her enemy, tore the mask from his face, and sent him to die in the closet where she had waited for twenty years. "Her expression as he went, and his tottering along on crutches toward the background were shocking and fascinating – this was great acting, a brilliant dramatist's powerful scene executed so that every strand of meaning and dramatic action stood out," Kragh-Jacobsen declared – and most other reviewers concurred.

Bergman's reading then counterpointed the mood of this unremittingly bleak climax with the lighter, conciliatory tone of the Mummy's thematically crucial speech about human compassion and atonement ("I can wipe out the past, undo what is done.") This passage – accentuated in the Malmö performance "as a breathing space that pointed ahead toward the third act"[29] – provided a touchstone for the director's structural image of the play as a progression towed purification and redemption. In his subsequent revival at Dramaten, which in so many other respects differed radically from its predecessor, the Mummy's second-act speech continued to hold the key to his thinking about the work – to the extent that it even prompted him to reassign the play's closing words of benediction and peace to the Mummy as well. During rehearsals for this production, he commented: "In the end, I have stressed the fact that the only thing that can give us any kind of salvation – a secular salvation – is the grace and compassion that come out of ourselves."[30] Even a brief excerpt from the production script illustrates the intricate manner in which a key speech such as this was choreographed and orchestrated into a word-melody in the Bergman performance:

THE MUMMY (*Frankly and seriously*) But *I* can stop time in its its course. *I* can wipe out the past (*Looks at the Colonel*) and undo what is done.
  (*The Colonel, the Fiancé, and the Baron raise their eyes to the Mummy. The Mummy crosses to the clock, lays a hand on the dial. The ticking stops*)
THE MUMMY Not with bribes, not with hatred. But through suffering . . . and repentance.
  (*The projection of a brick wall* [which had appeared earlier on Hummel's sarcastic lines about "this estimable house"] *dims*)
  (*The Mummy crosses down behind the Colonel, lays hold of him, looks at Hummel. The Colonel takes her hand*)
THE MUMMY We *are* poor, miserable creatures, we know that. We *have* erred, we *have* transgressed, like all the rest. We *are* not what we seem to be. At bottom we are better than ourselves, since *we* abhor and detest our misdeeds. (*Crosses down behind Hummel. Spitefully, fighting back tears*) But with you, Jacob Hummel, with your false name . . .
  (*The Colonel, the Fiancé, and the Baron begin again to raise their heads*)

THE MUMMY...come here to sit in judgment, *that* proves that you are more
    contemptible . . .
    (*The brick wall projection vanishes. The chairs in the round salon* [on which the
    characters are seated] *are lighted very strongly from the back and the front*)
THE MUMMY...than we are. And you . . . you . . . you are not the one you seem
    to be. [. . .][31]

Bergman conceived the lattice of dynamic human relationships into
which he divided the ghost supper scene – for example, the bond of tenderness and loyalty between the Mummy and the Colonel, the continuously oscillating struggle between Hummel and his victims, the dual role
of the Mummy as both prosecutor and executioner – primarily in terms of
concrete, suggestive patterns of physical movement, gesture, lighting, and
sound. "Remember, we are not playing psychological theatre," he told his
cast at Dramaten. "The rhythm of the play is fundamentally important.
Here there are no connecting links as in Ibsen's plays, which are much
easier to act. Here you have to turn on a dime."[32] The aggressiveness
and sheer emotional vehemence with which these relationships were delineated in the 1973 revival set that performance distinctly apart from its
predecessor in Malmö. In particular, the intense, Shylock-like Hummel
of Toivo Pawlo was not the tottering, shattered giant that Benkt-Åke
Benktsson had created twenty years earlier. Strindberg's stage directions
describe the old man in the black frock coat as basically passive, shriveled
up "like a dying insect" once his past is brought to light. By contrast,
Pawlo's image of Hummel was a poisonous pistachio-green spider who
fought actively and desperately to the last, and who had finally to be
dragged to his extermination by Johansson, the servant whom he had
enslaved by blackmail.

When the Mummy (Gertrud Fridh) ordered Hummel into the closet
to hang himself, he attempted several steps without his crutches, fell,
and then rolled sprawling on the floor in an effort to escape, uttering
unintelligible noises all the while. Johansson, seeing his slavery at an end,
leaped brutally on his struggling master, dragged him bodily into the
closet, and shut it. Cold light filled the stage as Bengtsson, portrayed in
this production as an old enemy of Hummel's, put up the death screen
before the closet door and then stepped ominously behind it. A snapping
sound was heard from the closet, followed by a death rattle; the Mummy,
who opened the closet door and looked inside to be certain, spoke her
lines to the others ("It is finished. May God have mercy on his soul")
with quiet satisfaction. Their "Amen" was not spoken in unison, as the
text prescribes, but was instead repeated in turn by the Colonel, the

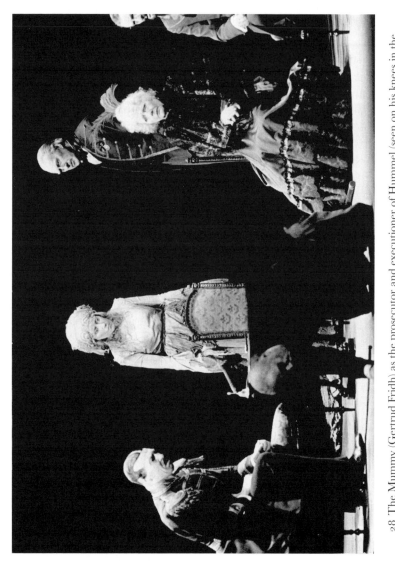

28 The Mummy (Gertrud Fridh) as the prosecutor and executioner of Hummel (seen on his knees in the foreground) in Bergman's 1973 revival of *The Ghost Sonata* at Dramaten.

Fiancé, Bengtsson, and then "very brightly" by the Baron. "It must not become too ritualistic," Bergman cautioned. When the final Amen was uttered, the sound of harp tones broke in as the Young Lady, seated in the background with Arkenholz, began to accompany the first of his two recitations of the so-called Song of the Sun.[33]

It might be said that Bergman had prepared the audience for the brutality of Hummel's slaughter by the excruciating sequence he composed to illustrate, in concrete terms, the virtual savagery of Hummel's own "unmasking" of the Colonel, played by Anders Ek in an almost caricatured parade-dress uniform of scarlet and gold braid. What is in the text a short, rather inert speech about stripping the pretentious Colonel naked became a starkly physical torture scene that the old man enjoyed prolonging:

HUMMEL (*Leaps up, pushes the Colonel down on a chair that overturns, leaving the Colonel on the floor*) Take off that hair of yours!

COLONEL (*On his knees, groans and obeys*)

HUMMEL (*Points*) Have a look at yourself in the mirror! Take out your false teeth while you're at it! Tear off that moustache! (*The Colonel obeys. Hummel thrusts him over to the left*)

HUMMEL Let Bengtsson (*slits up the Colonel's uniform so that a corset is exposed*) unlace your metal corset . . .

COLONEL (*Closes his eyes*)

HUMMEL . . . and then we shall see if a certain valet Mr. XYZ won't recognize himself! A valet who used to flirt with the maid in order to scrounge in a certain kitchen!

COLONEL (*Takes hold of the bell on the table and rings*)

HUMMEL (*Grasps the Colonel by the neck and pushes him so that he falls forward on his knees*) Don't touch that bell! If you call Bengtsson, I'll have him arrested! (*The clock strikes six*)

HUMMEL (*Standing over the Colonel with his crutch*) Here come the guests! [. . .][34]

At that point the terrorized and decimated officer crawled on his knees to the table and began to replace his social mask – his wig, his glued-on moustache, his false teeth – before the eyes of the audience. Seldom has the critical commonplace "spiritual striptease" acquired such tangible reality in a theatre. "When this overstuffed peacock with his centre-parted wig, stupidly slack jaw, and a waxed moustache that resembles a question mark is stripped bare before our very eyes by Hummel, he is transformed into miserable, quivering human wreckage," Leif Zern declared in *Dagens Nyheter* (January 14, 1973).

It is not, of course, the macabre universe of the Ghost Supper in itself that constitutes the severest challenge to a director undertaking

Strindberg's *Sonata*, but rather the requirement that the mood of this dark middle movement must be convincingly integrated into the overall melodic pattern. In Bergman's earlier production at the Malmö City Theatre, the immense proportions of the space itself further complicated the problem. By reducing both the seating capacity and the proscenium opening by more than one-third and building the stage out into the auditorium, however, he succeeded in creating an unexpectedly intimate atmosphere in the vast theatre. Special light towers installed behind the proscenium at either side of the stage provided sculptural backlighting for the actors and also facilitated the use of the projections upon which the scenography of Martin Ahlbom depended. The first of Ahlbom's scenes bore the clearest mark of the Molander influence: "Not the walls of Karlaplan 10 – that would have been copying – but at any rate a totally realistic Östermalm prospect with banal doorway statues on guard outside the aristocratic residence, with the advertisement pillar and drinking fountain, with Oscar's Church seen in the background, and with church chimes and steamship bells as atmospheric sound effects," Per Erik Wahlund wrote in *Svenska Dagbladet* (March 6, 1954). Yet although there was nothing abstract or obviously "strange" about the milieu into which the Student innocently wandered, both the lighting and the actions of the characters moving about the large, film-grey house evoked a distinctly hallucinatory ambience. As the scheming "soul stealer" Hummel told the Student about the unfortunate inhabitants of the Colonel's establishment and "they appeared in their windows, nodding, laughing, watering flowers," they seemed to form what *Stockholms Tidningen* called "a perfectly staged marionette number. Hummel sits at the outer edge of the stage as the oddly calculating director."

This metatheatrical sense of a play being enacted within the play, for the specific benefit of Arkenholz, was an integral element in Bergman's interpretation of *The Ghost Sonata* as – at this stage in his thinking, at least – the waking dream of the clairvoyant Student. The director employed various devices to strengthen this impression. One of them was to dissociate the "dreamer" from the other characters in terms of tone, makeup, gesture, and general appearance – an idea that, while often used before, inevitably seems to create its share of critical confusion. Lighting effects, projections of swirling "mind-mist," and even a transparent scrim that hung throughout the performance "like a barely visible veil separating the stage reality and the auditorium" (Wahlund) all conspired to maintain the impression of a dream.

The basic concept of the play as the Student's dream did not, however, fully succeed in welding the "difficult" third movement – the traditional stumbling block in most interpretations – to the rest of the composition. "Life is terrible, and we must toil through it. But since it is at bottom only a nightmare, dreamed in this case by the young student, the last human being in a dying world, then there is redemption to be found beyond time and space," Nils Beyer contended in *Morgon-Tidningen* (March 6). But many of the other critics took a different view. The poetic tone of the last part, Kragh-Jacobsen maintained, "is finely conceived, but it is dramatically pale – besides which it follows the bitterest of Strindberg's denunciations of life's most banal vexations." Deliberate paleness seemed in fact to dominate the setting – a severe white interior in elegant *Jugendstil*, furnished chiefly with denotative object-symbols: a white harp (frozen music), a marble statue (petrified beauty), a slender white chair (loneliness), and the obligatory image of Buddha.[35] Bergman banished the vision of Böcklin's painting at the end, choosing instead to punctuate the play's progression toward purification and atonement with a more accessibly human – though perhaps no more dramatically logical – visual effect. In a final tableau, Folke Sundquist's Arkenholz drew aside the death screen once more in order to take the Young Lady's head in his hands. "The lights went down on the Student holding Gaby Stenberg's magnificent face in his lap," Ebbe Linde recorded in *Dagens Nyheter* (March 6). One of his colleagues even thought he caught a glimpse of a single ray of golden sunlight playing on the young man's face.

It was clearly his own sense of dissatisfaction with this approach to the final act of *The Ghost Sonata* that animated the radically revised interpretation staged by Bergman at Dramaten in 1973. The accomplishment of three basic objectives seemed to underlie his new approach: the forging of an organic relationship between the last act and the rest of the play; the articulation of a less artificially "symbolic" and hence more meaningful resolution to the last act, in line with his concept of "secular salvation"; finally but not least, the adoption of a much more simplified, actor-oriented style of production. The first two of these objectives are related to the specific play itself. The third point, however, is more general and relates to the overall change in outlook and method that was so strikingly apparent in Bergman's radically demystified, chamber-play adaptation of *A Dream Play* in 1970. In the case of his new *Sonata* three years later, the play was performed on a virtually bare stage stripped of every object and every item of scenery that might, in the director's opinion, "block the action or make it heavy." His designer, Marik Vos, created a permanent, completely open acting arena enclosed in a semicircle by two towering, almost Craig-like screens. Low risers at the sides and a higher, raked platform that connected the screens at the back flanked this neutral space. Two significant objects were positioned at either side of the proscenium, as suggestive physical reminders (not symbols) of key psychological impulses in Bergman's interpretation. One was an antique standing clock whose ticking proclaimed the relentless passage of Time, which the Mummy is able to stop temporarily in the second act. The other object was the marble statue of a beautiful young woman, a reminder of the Mummy as she once was in the past, just as she is in the present what the Young Lady, her daughter and alter ego, is destined to become.

Other objects were used with extreme economy, and their rigorously symmetrical placement underlined the basic thematic relationship of one act to another. In the first movement only Hummel's wheelchair and the street fountain at which the Milkmaid offers the Student a drink of water stood on the empty stage; in the last movement these were replaced, in precisely the same relative positions, by a slender white chair in which the Student sits and the white harp and chair of the Young Lady. Contrastingly heavy black chairs stood in a sombre semicircle in the Colonel's salon for the fateful supper. In general, however, human figure composition rather than scenery became the raw material in Bergman's directorial concept for this version of *The Ghost Sonata*. "The important thing is what happens to the bodies," he declared in rehearsal. "No furnishings that overshadow the action, nothing that stands around anywhere unless [it contributes to] a choreographic pattern that must be able to move with complete freedom in relation to space and scenery. Nothing must get in the way."[36] Åke Perlström provided a very observant comment on this strategy in *Göteborgs-Posten* (January 14): "The characters are at all times forcefully liberated from the setting. They stand close together on the forestage, and we perceive them in closeups. Stronger than this, concentration can hardly become."

In most instances, lighting and projections on the two concave screens and on a cyclorama in the background took the place of actual scenery. Originally Bergman even conceived of the marble statue and the standing clock as projections; ultimately he attenuated the tangible reality of these two properties by using projected shadows of palm fronds that played over them. In the first act, the projections of an actual turn-of-the-century

Stockholm house and church facade might have seemed yet another reiteration of the familiar Molander view of Karlaplan 10. But Bergman's deconstructed approach to the play soon adjusted such an impression. The *same* film-grey house facade projected on each of the mammoth thirty-two foot screens evoked the half-real feeling of a dream. Moreover, during Hummel's descriptions of the blighted fates of the residents, both he and Arkenholz faced the audience continuously, thus locating the imaginary house in the auditorium (where, at the same time, the audience continued to look at a distorted mirror image of the house behind the actors). Typically, Bergman justified this Pirandellian tactic in purely practical terms, as a device that made the audience better able to see the faces and reactions of the actors. Just as typically, a number of critics were inclined to see deeper significance in it: "We, the audience, are like the bogus colonel and the other inhabitants of the house – counterfeits with ugly secrets and a guilt-ridden past," the critic from *Sydsvenska Dagbladet Snällposten* suggested.

Like the house and church in the first act, both the heavy, picture-cluttered interior for the Colonel's supper party and the high, drapery-festooned windows that signified the claustrophobic Hyacinth Room were projections, characterized by the same soft, dreamlike diffuseness of focus. At one point Bergman had intended to project gradually withering hyacinths as an "illustration" of the Young Lady's chamber, but his determination to exclude illustrative projection reflected his over-all resistance to overt, directly attached symbolism in the production. Ultimately, only the bluish white lighting of the scene and the hyacinth blue of the Young Lady's dress were used to suggest what Bergman conceived of as "a sense that she has surrounded herself with a barrier of colour and warmth and fragrance."[37] Suggestion was also the essence of a visual image that recurred at a crucial point in each of the acts, when the projection denoting place (street, round salon, hyacinth room) faded and was replaced by a purely connotative projection of a high, shadowy brick wall. This happened at the moment when the Milkmaid whom Hummel has presumably drowned emerged (from a trap in the stage floor) before his eyes, when Hummel began his denunciation of the supper guests, and yet again when the Student began to lash out at the decay of the house and of Adèle. The implications of the wall image were multiple and unattached to "meaning" as such, but the image lent graphic substantiation tot the Student's outcry about "this penal colony, madhouse, and morgue of a world."

29 The projection of the shadowy brick wall as it appeared on two high screens that framed Marik Vos' minimalist setting for the Hyacinth Room in Bergman's 1973 production.

As had been the case in the Malmö production, projections were again used to sustain a dreamlike atmosphere during the brief intervals needed for changes of scene and costume. In this instance, however, a much more abstract "snowfall" comprised of rising and falling dots of light projected on an opaque front curtain took the place of the cinematic "mind-mists" seen in the previous version. Regarding the identity of the dreamer of this dream play, however, a more fundamental change had taken place in Bergman's thinking. It is perfectly possible to identify the Poet in *A Dream Play* as Strindberg's alter ego and then proceed, as Bergman had done in his production of that play three years earlier, to present him as its connecting and controlling consciousness; it is less easy to view the Student in *The Ghost Sonata* in this way. "No, it is Strindberg himself who is the dreamer," Bergman had decided in his new performance. "Notice the inward movement of the play, from the street to the round salon and finally to the hyacinth room. Strindberg takes us by the hand and leads us ever deeper into the dream."[38] The idea of the author's "presence" was in fact not pursued in any detail, but a fleeting visual sign of it was an out-of-focus image of the elder Strindberg that materialized on the front curtain between the second and third acts.

In itself, of course, a visual effect such as this would do little to accomplish what one must take to be the primary objective of this reinterpretation – namely, to forge an organic link between the play's first two acts and its potentially anticlimactic final movement. The theatrical solution that Bergman offered to this dramaturgical problem was radical and, to some minds, even extreme. As a solution designed primarily to clarify *emotional* responses for the actors, it found expression mainly in a reconfiguration of internal character relationships rather than in external visual or aural effects. "The fact that the Young Lady is slowly turning into another Mummy is the fundamental idea in my production," Bergman has said. "That is what is so horrifying about the whole situation." While this idea in itself is not so startling, the result it led to was. At first Bergman had evidently intended to let the actors who played the Mummy and Hummel also take the parts of the Young Lady and the Student in the last act. Ultimately, only the female half of this remarkable twinning operation was put into practice, and the versatile Gertrud Fridh (helped by a nonspeaking stand-in as needed) assumed the demanding double role of mother and daughter. The Mummy of the middle act thus became the Young Lady of the first and last movements. Mathias Henrikson's Arkenholz was also provided with enough facial resemblance to the Hummel of Toivo Pawlo (beard, moustache, eyeglasses) to suggest the director's view that the Student is in reality a Hummel in embryo: "He is no longer the pure-hearted young man who dashes on the stage at the beginning. In that he has taken Hummel's hand, he is initiated."[39]

These role realignments brought about in turn a full-scale reassessment of the basic tone and emotional relationships of the difficult final movement of the sonata. "In the third act, Bergman believes, we are led into the deepest part of the dream, the infantile, where all normal proportions have ceased to operate," Åke Janzon wrote in *Svenska Dagbladet*. "The intense aspirations and the everyday torments of human life are here compressed into a single scene of exorcism, supplication, damnation, lamentation, and lyricism." Perlström's fine analysis in *Göteborgs-Posten* came straight to the emotional point of the Mummy's transfiguration. "She returns again in the third act, the same person trapped in the daughter's destiny, to become a new sacrificial victim. The Student, the young hero of the first acts, cannot help her; on the contrary he drives her to her death with his absolute demands. He has in fact taken on the role of Hummel, and the Colonel reaches out toward his dead daughter as someone might stretch out a hand to a drowning person."

At the core of Bergman's theatrical paraphrase of the text is a statement he made to his cast at an early rehearsal:

And this we must bear in mind continually, that the Student kills the Young Lady. And this is an unpleasant and terrifying scene of unmasking and murder. It corresponds to the unmasking of Hummel by the Mummy in the second act, but here it is enormously much more freed of every shred of reality . . . Here it is only with ugly words that he touches her, he makes violent gestures toward her, doesn't he, he seizes hold of her, he tears off her clothing. And this kills her.[40]

"That 'doesn't he' is truly disarming," Strindberg scholar Gunnar Brandell later asserted. "Not many would in reality go along with the validity of this interpretation, yet not anyone in Bergman's ensemble seems to have registered a divergent opinion." Brandell goes on to support a more traditional interpretation of the Young Lady's death: in addition to the Hummels of this world, there are in Strindberg also "human beings of a more delicate fibre, who never have been able to harden themselves to live, to withstand the truth of life." The Young Lady is one of these, Brandell argues, and thus "her death in the third part is intended as a liberation, a wandering into the Böcklin picture toward a nothingness that is worth far more than blood, dirt, and tears." As for the Student, he is "the wanderer, perhaps the poet, standing halfway outside as so many figures in Strindberg do, with traces of the Good Samaritan and perhaps even of Christ," this critic suggests. He does not join the living dead nor does he die at all, because "he is essentially just a student on a field trip to 'this penal colony, madhouse, and morgue of a world.' "[41] This critic's view of the play's "meaning" found, in fact, neither support nor contradiction in Bergman's much more open and allusive performance interpretation, which was concerned mainly with orchestrating the emotional beats in a work in which faith in language as a guide to truth and meaning has all but collapsed, and words are able to be used as deadly weapons in a psychological conflict that Strindberg earlier described as "psychic murder." "The interpretation must begin with the last act. If you do this, everything falls into place," Bergman explained in a pre-production interview in *Svenska Dagbladet* (December 12, 1972). "The logic of everyday consciousness must cease to function in the third act, because an entirely different kind of logic that is much more drastic and frightening prevails here." In this nightmarish context, he continues, "the Student murders the Young Lady, little by little, with words."

A suggestive rhythmic pattern of movement, gesture, intonation, and tempo changes charted the transitions in this process, from the tenderness of the hyacinth poetry to the bitterness of the household concerns introduced by the Cook's intrusion and back to the tenderness of the final benediction. Gertrud Fridh's performance was a virtuoso demonstration of the Young Lady's gradual "mummification." "She develops backwards," Leif, Zern observed in *Dagens Nyheter* (January 14, 1973). "The role of the mother is taken over by her step by step in a process that the actress reproduces with alarming precision." She and her director devised a vocabulary of expressively repetitive gestures to reinforce the growing resemblance of the Young Lady to her grotesque parrot–parent. When she had to answer a question, for example, Fridh thrust her head out in front of her shoulders, while her hands fluttered helplessly up under her chin. At other times, her fingertips were seen pressed against her forehead as her hands covered her face – a movement, one reviewer observed, "in which the full impression of a sleepwalker on the verge of the fatal wakening is concentrated" (*Göteborgs Handels- och Sjöfartstidning*, January 15).

The appearance of the monstrous Cook, who "belongs to the Hummel family of vampires" and cannot be dismissed, touched off the final disintegration. As the desperation of the Student and the defensive "mummy" gestures of the Young Lady grew more emphatic, a cold, harsh light began to dominate the forestage. The long monologue with which Arkenholz "murders" Adèle began as a purely verbal threat, made menacing by his alternating moves of approach and withdrawal. The projection of the brick wall replaced the hyacinth room interior on the screens as a direct visual response to the Student's bitter description of the madhouse where his father died for truth. But it also carried broader connotations in Bergman's conception: "The Student and the Young Lady are now in the same prison in which the others – those who have deformed them – have lived all their lives," he explained. "They are locked together in a kind of hell, and it is not until she dies that the air and light return."[42]

The wall projection, silently proclaiming the prison-house in which the young couple found themselves, signaled an emotional peripety in the Student's monologue, which now acquired a new tone of increased aggressiveness ("If you keep silent too long, stagnant water accumulates, and things begin to rot. That's what is happening in this house.)" His struggle to regain the air and the light became more physical and more overtly violent – while, on the platform in the background, the Colonel and the Mummy (i.e., Fridh's stand-in) began for the first time to take notice of the events occurring in front of them, in the Hyacinth Room. The Student's implied sexual challenge to the Young Lady ("speaking of which, where can one find virginity?") marked another important transition, given savage physical expression by this Arkenholz, who brutally spread her thighs and thrust his hand between her legs. The monologue reached its explosive climax on the key line that follows the Student's futile attempt to coax music from the mute harp ("To think that the most beautiful flowers are so poisonous.)" At this juncture, in a paroxysm of anger and frustration, he dragged his adversary forcibly to the front of the stage in a manner that recalled Hummel's similar treatment of the Colonel. As she, too, sank to her knees in anguish, her hyacinth-blue dress tore loose and fell from her in tatters. Beneath it she wore a ragged and soiled undergarment in greyish white – virtually a mummy's winding sheet – streaked with red down the sides and in the outlines of the crotch.

Unmasked and literally put to death by the lacerating truths the Student has compelled her to hear ("There are poisons that seal the eyes and poisons that open them"), the Young Lady called for the death screen as the wall projection vanished, leaving an empty background bathed in the soft, mild light of liberation (the equivalent of Strindberg's problematic direction that "the room vanishes"). In view of the conception of the Student as the Young Lady's "murderer," he was poorly suited to be the speaker of the closing lines of consolation to her – and one of the most interesting choices in this performance was to divide these concluding lines between the Colonel and the Mummy. The Colonel, who had undergone a startling change from the stylish, scarlet-uniformed martinet of the second act to a Beckettian old man in a worn grey bathrobe and slippers, spoke the first part of the speech ("Your liberator is coming – welcome, pale and gentle one") as he quietly and affectionately covered Adèle with the screen. All religious references were excised from this moment of purely secular salvation, however, and the only Buddhist intimation was created by such suggestions as the old man's mild tone of resignation and his humble sitting position on the stage floor. Henrikson's Student again spoke the Song of the Sun, but the poem's tone of optimistic affirmation was consistently undercut by his sarcastic reading of it, reflecting Bergman's own conviction that the poem is ultimately "nonsense" for a contemporary audience. "If the Student reads the poem with a skeptical tone the second time, it seems to me meaningful," the director explained. "Every second comment in that verse seems dubious. And especially after Strindberg himself gives a brilliant demonstration of man's gruesomeness and madness, I think it is quite right that the Student reaches this conclusion."[43] Unlike the Malmö production, no touching tableau was struck and no ray of sunlight played on Arkenholz's face. After finishing his recital, he repeated the last word of the poem ("innocent") with utter disbelief in his voice, and then simply walked away into the darkness.

In this performance, the Mummy spoke Strindberg's final words of consolation, and the effect thus created became one of its most arresting moments. Concealed by the death screen, from behind which an outstretched female arm protruded, Fridh was able to exchange places with her stand-in and resume her Mummy costume during the delivery of the Song of the Sun (certainly one valid reason for retaining this troublesome speech). As Arkenholz concluded his poem, the Mummy entered. Slowly, she removed the death screen to reveal the prostrate form behind it. As harp music sounded from an unseen Toten Insel, she spoke the closing lines of benediction over "this child of the world of disappointments, guilt, suffering, and death" – in essence, a benediction over the corpse of her former self. "The third act no longer appears a romantic appendage to the first two acts," Zern wrote in *Dagens Nyheter*. Rather, the harsh and bitter tone of the Ghost Supper, "where the phases of bourgeois family life are depicted and laid bare by a Strindberg more furious than ever before," reasserted itself "according to the eternal law of repetition . . . The truly fascinating thing about this solution is that it reshapes the play into a whole in which everything is accomplished with remorseless dramatic logic."

That this "reshaping" process encountered its share of opposition from literary critics is perhaps to be expected. *The Ghost Sonata*, Brandell argued in the article cited earlier, "is not constructed according to the principle: three steps to hell. It seems to be a triptych in which each section has its own mood and its own theme, regardless of the fact that Strindberg lets many threads run on through the entire weave." Therefore, this critic reasons, by attempting to introduce dramatic progression and continuity ("an almost unbroken crescendo") into his performance, a director such as Bergman (or Molander or Reinhardt, one might add) "goes his own way and uses Strindberg's text [to create] a dramatic structure of a fundamentally different character." Accordingly, Brandell goes on, by subordinating either the vacillating, desultory movement of this play or the repetitive circularity of *To Damascus* to "a straight line, a steadily increasing intensity, ever stronger and more unsettling dream effects," Bergman had made a sacrifice: "something of the atmosphere, the heaviness, the wearisome *tedium vitae* also disappears."

Yet the interpretative function of the director must surely be to translate the explicit or implicit choices and values he or she discovers in a text into the language of the theatre – which is, after all, the only language in which a play *can* be heard by a living, contemporary audience. The act of producing a play on the stage creates a new organism, an integral work of art responsive, by definition, to a whole new set of circumstances. From the work of Lindberg, Vakhtangov, Reinhardt, and the German expressionist directors of the twenties to Lepage, Wilson, and Bergman in our own day, the Strindberg productions we have been considering have all been stylizations. Style, wrote Fuerst and Hume in 1929 in their classic exposition of modernist staging, "is not the indiscriminate application of a preconceived idea to any play whatsoever; it lies in a unity of conception in which all the stage elements represent the work of the author in a manner that satisfies *the receptivity of the epoch*."[44] Precisely in these terms, these Strindberg stylizations represent a broader, ongoing movement, inspired by the challenge of the post-Inferno works and aimed at perceiving them from a new perspective, for a new audience and a new age. "When a work outlives its geographical and historical boundaries," the Italian director Giorgio Strehler observed of classical revivals in general, "the original author–audience relationship is severed immediately, to be reassembled later in a different manner. The nature of the audience changes, and consequently the nature of the author changes."[45]

"In my case, it has always been a matter of reading closely. And interpreting in the same way a conductor interprets a score," Bergman has said more than once. "I want only to present the play and make it live in the hearts of the audience." His successive reinterpretations of *The Ghost Sonata* have differed in many respects, but his objective has remained the same – to materialize the *experience* of Strindberg's oneiric fantasy in the intuitive imagination of the audience, rather than in its conscious intellect. No modern director has realized better than Bergman that the spectator's direct emotional responsiveness to a text – particularly a text such as this one – presumes, above all, a mutual consent that he invariably seeks and obtains by the simplest means. The emphasis on faces and figure compositions in his actor-oriented approach exerts, in turn, a pressure from the stage toward the audience that eliminates all distance. Perhaps no Strindberg performance in recent years has provided a better illustration of the force of this direct and unmitigated contact between the audience and the living actors than his latest revisitation of Strindberg's most difficult chamber play.

THE GHOST SONATA IN THE CONTEMPORARY THEATRE

While it was Robert Wilson who ushered *A Dream Play* into the new millennium with his contemplative "installation" of it, it was, appropriately enough, Ingmar Bergman who performed the same service for *The Ghost Sonata* with his bare-stage revival of the play in Målarsalen (The Paint Shop), Dramaten's intimate studio theatre, in February 2000. Some other interesting performances have continued to appear during the past quarter of a century, ranging in stylishness from the colourful, aestheticized experiments staged by Henri Ronse at the Odéon in Paris in 1975 and Andrei Serban at the Yale Rep in 1977 to the darkly postmodernist reinterpretation presented at the Betty Nansen Theatre in Copenhagen by Staffan Valdemar Holm in 1989. The new Bergman version stood out, however, in a much more emphatic way, as a definitive turning point both in his ongoing dialogue with this play and in its performance history in general. Seen widely on tour, his "exquisite, hideous and altogether stunning production" succeeded at last in persuading even the New York critics of the irresistible force of what the *New York Times* (June 22, 2001) extolled as Strindberg's "fantasia on moral corruption and deceit," from which "even as you flinch, you are unlikely to look away."

The ruling image in Bergman's new performance was decay – physical decay, moral decay, the decay and death of ideals and dreams. "Seldom has cosmic disgust filled a stage so ravishingly," Ben Brantley remarked in *The Times* review. This concept found particularly vivid expression in the grotesque, almost Hogarth-like details of physical characterization that abounded. For example, when the elegant Dark Lady lifted her veil, the audience saw a large, festering growth on her face that she continually tried to conceal. The bogus Baron compulsively licked a bleeding sore on his mouth. Hummel's cast-off Fiancée displayed an oversize red ear that made her painful flirtatiousness seem all the more absurd. And the Young Lady was, in Elin Klinga's widely admired performance, inescapably part of this gallery of dead souls and lost causes from the beginning. A beautiful young woman with blank, lifeless eyes, she seemed a doomed, Miss Julie kind of figure whose graceful movements gradually deteriorated into twitches and spasms. During much of the first act, she sat in a corner of the stage as a watching presence, tending a window box of wilted hyacinths by pouring perfume over their dead stalks.

Bergman's choice of the spatial intimacy of Målarsalen, which seats fewer than 200 spectators, returned the play to the chamber-theatre format for which Strindberg had intended it. Here, however, Göran Wassberg's stage design made no use whatsoever of scenery as such. The stage was an unlocalized playing area bounded by neutral black rehearsal screens. Projections of old houses appeared like faded photographs and then disappeared again, but no attempt was made to create an illusion of "place," as Bergman had done in previous productions of the play. His new version, Leif Zern commented in *Dagens Nyheter* (February 13, 2000) "is an entirely different story. It has moved the drama to an interior stage" where "everything that happens does so through the imagination." Rich nuances of colour and texture in the lighting and costumes translated themselves in the spectator's mind into changing moods and locations. Prominent in their isolation, two objects stood at opposite sides of the empty stage as permanent iconic reminders of the dualism in Bergman's vision of *The Ghost Sonata*: the idealized beauty of a nude statue of a young woman stood juxtaposed with the uncompromising reality of passing time, in the shape of a ticking grandfather clock. In the opening minutes of the play, an analogous polarity was suggested in a much more direct and shocking way. The pure and cleansing water that the Milkmaid gives the Student came, in this instance, not from a fountain but from a small covered hole in the stage floor. Only moments later, the Caretaker's Wife emerged to dump a pailful of the house's waste into an identical hole at the other side of the stage. Strong as such an image was, however, it remained an open, ambivalent suggestion. As Michael Feingold remarked in a review in *The Village Voice* (July 4–10, 2001), "Bergman's fierce specificity turned out to share the play's ambiguous richness."

Following Strindberg's example in the program for the original production at Intima teatern, Bergman also subtitled his version "A Fantasy." The active imaginative involvement of his audience was further strengthened by the absence in Målarsalen of any separation between stage and auditorium. The audience here found itself *inside* the house, looking out as Hummel (Jan Malmsjö) told its secrets to the Student (Jonas Malmsjö), while the Caretaker's Wife (Gertrud Mariano) obsessively polished the brass around the "doorway" at the front of the acting area. "Nothing was shown on the stage. We see no facade, and through this mirror inversion of inside and outside . . . the play's focus can be located both in their consciousness and in ours," Zern observed. In a more specific sense, however, the fantasy seemed to unfold in the imagination of Jonas Malmsjö's sympathetic young Student, whose nightmare of shattered hopes and bitter disappointments it so clearly was. As the lights came up slowly at the beginning of the play, he seemed to awaken from sleep, rubbed his eyes and temples, and crawled forward to be helped to his feet by the silent Milkmaid. After her ministrations and departure, however, he lay down again to rest ("I'm still half asleep"), only to be deliberately reawakened by Hummel's intrusive first line ("Excuse my asking . . .") Then, as the figures from the house came alive to the mocking accompaniment of hurdy-gurdy music, the nightmare within the dream began.

The Malmsjös, father and son in real life, played effectively on a growing sense of sinister paternalism in the relationship in which the Old Man tried to enmesh the Student. His piercing eyes and shaven head hidden in the opening scene by dark glasses and a fur toque, Jan Malmsjö's Hummel seemed to exert a virtually supernatural power over the actions and sounds in the shadow world in which Arkenholz suddenly found himself. "Of course one can detect a self-reflexive point of view in the directorial concept: Hummel is the master director who will make a whole house dance to his tune. But the metaphysical, Mephistophelean dimension is more obvious," Lars Ring remarked in his review in *Svenska Dagbladet* of the Swedish premiere. When this subtle Strindbergian tempter felt his physical and psychic hold on his quarry beginning to slip ("Let go of my hand – you are draining me of all my strength"), he quickly invoked his strongest inducement – the dreamlike apparition of the lovely Young Lady, who entered through the audience, unexpectedly kissed the astounded Arkenholz, and soon took her place as another watching character at the edge of the stage. Here, she was in turn continually watched by the clairvoyant but in this case blindly infatuated Student. If the play became "his dream of the possibilities life offers," as Donald Lyons suggested in his review in the *New York Post* (June 22, 2001), the grotesque juxtaposition of Elin Klinga's inwardly dead beauty with her manifestly dead hyacinths left no doubt in the audience's mind about the ultimate futility of all such dreams.

Although Hummel ruled this realm of deceit and false appearances, Bergman's mise-en-scène also stressed the presence of his victims as a retributive force that would ultimately bring about his downfall. The angry ghost of the murdered Milkmaid, danced by Virpi Pahkinen "like a physical scream from a Munch painting" (Ring), became the visual embodiment of this theme of revenge. Her attack on Hummel at the end of the first movement was a violent onslaught that he fought off with equal violence, killing her again. At the Ghost Supper, however, she was waiting in the closet to pull him in and drop the noose around his neck. The two servants provided willing assistance on this occasion. Örjan Ramberg played Johansson as a darkly comic, dangerously obsequious lackey who, when his chance for freedom came, literally carried his incoherent master to his destruction behind the screen. Bengtsson, at one time Hummel's servant but at another time his master, emerged as a fascinating mixture of rococo butler, Beckettian clown, and brutal executioner in Erland Josephson's rendering. The tasks of arranging chairs for the Colonel's supper party and arranging the death screen for Hummel's extermination were performed by him with the same unsettlingly cool, ironic detachment.

As the Mummy, Hummel's most poignant victim and most forceful adversary, Gunnel Lindblom brought a new sense of determination and even premeditation to the deadly encounter for which she had waited so long. Underlying the strife and bitterness inherent in her personal relationship with her lost love was a deeper kind of anguish, aptly characterized by the critic for *Upsala Nya Tidning* (February 14) as "a life's sorrow that sprang from a lifetime of deception, and that carried existential overtones that were clearly heard throughout the performance." Wearing a moldering, shroud-like garment with the colour of dried blood and whistling the Toreador's march from *Carmen* as she emerged from her closet, she consciously *played* the "mad parrot" routine for the benefit of the servants. Likewise, when she crept up behind Hummel as he knelt before her statue, her invented nonsense language of coos and squeals was a deliberate mockery of his empty sentimentality. Never, in other words, was the Mummy's Pirandellian mask of madness other than just that, a mask behind which the suffering face of an angry and determined woman remained discernible at all times. Hence, Lindblom's untraditional portrayal of this character revealed her denunciation, humiliation, and destruction of Hummel not as the result of an unexpected dramatic "transformation" of Amelia's character, but as a foregone conclusion that sprang from a consciousness of self she had never relinquished.

With its uninterrupted playing time of exactly 100 minutes, Bergman's new *Sonata* was a swiftly flowing stream of images, faces, and juxtaposed suggestions that aspired to the purely emotional continuity generated by the clashing dissonances of modern music. The model in this instance was Bela Bartok's "Music for Strings, Percussion, and Celesta" (1926), which provided an underlying musical accompaniment to the action. Redefined solely in terms of musical (thematic) progression, Bergman's production brought particularly fresh coherence to the third act by scoring it as a steady, insistent crescendo that recapitulated the play's cascading motifs – deception, disillusionment, existential disgust, the decay of love, the corruption of hope and innocence. There was no serenity in Bergman's direction of this final movement, no recourse to ritual, no physical setting to contain and contextualize the verbal and visceral combat into which the Student's initially poetic courtship of the Young Lady almost immediately degenerated. Like the Mummy and the Milkmaid, they too "danced" their roles. As they sat or knelt or grappled and wrestled on the floor, the choreographed anguish of their violent actions matched their frustrated attempts at verbal communication, reflecting what Zern called "Bergman's ability to transpose feelings into physical realities."

The only furniture on the stage during this scene were the two chairs occupied by the Mummy and the Colonel who, as the stage directions indicate, could be seen sitting impassively in the background. In this performance, however, the menacing figures of the Cook and Bengtsson were also visible presences who watched from the periphery and eventually invaded the scene to chant the Cook's mocking defiance ("You suck the life out of us, and we out of you") in unison. As he sensed himself becoming increasingly entrapped in the secrets of the Young Lady's domestic and personal hell, Arkenholz's mounting revulsion turned to desperation and bitter rage. As Bergman had evidently abandoned his previous stance that the Student deliberately "kills" Adèle, Jonas Malmsjö was left freer to develop a more human, vulnerable, and unusually sympathetic portrayal of this problematic character. His Arkenholz was (as the Colonel tells Hummel) a poet and a singer of songs who watched the horrendous events of the Ghost Supper from the safety of his seat in the background, at times jotting down his observations in a black notebook from which he subsequently recited his Song of the Sun. But once caught in the mutual torment of his own relationship with the Young Lady, he found himself an observer no longer. As he began for the first time to tell *his* story, the madness that had overtaken his father suddenly seemed very near. "In his long concluding monologues, delivered in contorted postures, he succeeded in calling forth a sense of that primeval darkness that made one leave this performance inwardly shaken," the critic for *Göteborgs-Posten* (February 14) observed.

In her frantic efforts to escape the physical pain inflicted by his words, Klinga's Adèle suddenly dropped to the floor and began to crawl about like some grotesque insect, pursued and mauled by the equally desperate

30 The death of the Young Lady, watched with different reactions by the Mummy (Gunnel Lindblom), the Student (Jonas Malmsjö, kneeling), and Bengtsson (Erland Josephson), in the new Bergman production of *The Ghost Sonata* at Dramaten in 2000.

truthteller. As his invective reached its climax ("Christ descended into hell, that was his pilgrimage on earth"), her white, high-necked dress came apart and fell from her like a discarded masquerade costume. The startling collision montage which ended his "dystopian dream play" (to borrow Lars Ring's clever phrase) was, in fact, not as unambiguously bleak as many of the reviewers suggested. As the Young Lady's death throes toppled the screen erected by Bengtsson and she collapsed into the Student's arms, the ghost of the Milkmaid came rolling down the stage to lie behind her in the same prostrate position. Freeing himself from the Young Lady and from the time-stopped world of the play in general, Arkenholz dashed out through the audience, his face that of a terrified dreamer who has just awakened from his nightmare. The Mummy spoke the final simple words of benediction, without the encumbering reprise of the Song of the Sun. After the Young Lady's corpse had been carried out and the Milkmaid was left alone on the empty stage, she rose to perform a slow, contorted sequence of moves and postures – an ambiguous war dance that seemed to proclaim the victim's agony (hers, the Young Lady's, the Mummy's), the satisfaction of having hung the hangman, perhaps even the possibility of peace and release from pain.

As this very free interpretation of Strindberg's ending indicates, Bergman's newest revisitation of *The Ghost Sonata* departed in radical ways from the mise-en-scène prescribed by the play's printed stage directions. Yet this production was an intensely faithful and entirely valid expression of the play's inner spirit and its author's deeply troubled outlook. After sixty years as a Strindberg director, Bergman was again ready to make new choices that would lift this play out of its earlier performance traditions (his own included) and into the present, as a text for a contemporary theatre audience. One such choice was the adoption of an utterly dematerialized style that dismantled the work's highly detailed and ostensibly realistic context, in order to disclose and accentuate its inner rhythm of intense, dissonant emotionality. Another of his key decisions was to transpose purely intellectual allusions – the Böcklin painting, Buddhist thought, the language of the flowers, and so on – into a suggestive, sensory syntax of choreographed movements, gestures, facial expressions, colours, sounds, and colliding images. By no means less important was his restoration of a chamber-play intimacy that thrust the action forward, all but eliminating the separation between actor and audience in order to engage the spectator's full imaginative participation. The shadowy presences of watching characters lingering at the edges of the action further deepened and complicated the metatheatrical nature of spectatorship in the performance.

The end result of such decisions as these was a transfiguration of *The Ghost Sonata* that reasserted both its modernity and its performability in the theatre of our own time. As such, it demonstrated yet again the larger ongoing process that has been the subject of this book – a process in which the apparent statement of a given text is continually transformed, through the direct encounter of actor and audience, into living representation. "No play can speak for itself," Peter Brook has warned us, and hence in the absence of such a process of transformation, a play "may not make a sound," as Brook says. As for Strindberg's part in this dialectic of repeated reinterpretation and renewal, his response can be heard in his famous statement (in his Third Letter to the Intimate Theatre) that "to be 'your own contemporary' must be the task of the artist who is ever growing, ever renewing himself." In the modern theatre it has been, above all, the major performances of his post-Inferno dramas that have continued to show us the remarkably resilient contemporaneity that this singular genius was so determined to retain.

NOTES

1 BEFORE INFERNO: STRINDBERG AND NINETEENTH-CENTURY THEATRE

1 *Open Letters to the Intimate Theatre*, trans. Walter Johnson (Seattle, 1967), p. 289. Subsequent references are given in the text, identified as *LIT*.
2 In his autobiography *The Son of a Servant*, trans. Evert Sprinchorn (Garden City, NY, 1966), p. 6.
3 "On Modern Drama and Modern Theatre," translated in *Playwrights on Playwriting*, ed. Toby Cole (New York, 1961), p. 17.
4 Zola's letter was published in *Politiken* (Copenhagen), December 19, 1887.
5 *Strindberg's Letters*, ed. and trans. Michael Robinson (Chicago and London, 1992), I, p. 259. Hereafter, as is customary, Strindberg's letters will normally be referenced in the text by date and addressee, in order to facilitate access to different collections of his correspondence. However, for the sake of uniformity the translation used will, whenever possible, be that of the Robinson edition. The standard Swedish edition of Strindberg's letters is: *Brev*, eds. Torsten Eklund and Björn Meidal, 19 vols. (Stockholm, 1948–94).
6 Letter to the members of the Intimate Theatre, April 23, 1908; cf. August Falck, *Fem år med Strindberg*, 2nd edn. (Stockholm, 1935), p. 207.
7 Translation of the Preface is from Michael Robinson's edition, *Miss Julie and Other Plays* (Oxford and New York, 1998).
8 Cf. Harry Jacobsen, *Strindberg i firsernes København* (Copenhagen, 1948), p. 136.
9 The entire review is reprinted in translation in Michael Meyer, *Strindberg: A Biography* (London, 1985), pp. 215–16.
10 Inga-Stina Ewbank, "Shakespeare and Strindberg: Influence as Insemination," *Shakespearean Continuations: Essays in Honour of E.A.J. Honigmann*, eds. John Batchelor, Tom Cain and Claire Lamont (London and New York, 1997), pp. 335, 339.

2 TOWARD A NEW THEATRE: *TO DAMASCUS*

1 Adolphe Appia, "Light and Space," *Directors on Directing*, eds. Toby Cole and Helen Krich Chinoy (Indianapolis, 1968), p. 145.

2 Letter dated April 8, 1889, not included in Robinson: *Brev*, eds. Eklund and Meidal, VII (Stockholm, 1961), p. 308.

3 The manuscript of Bloch's report, entitled "Beretning om Shakespeare-scenen i München," is found among his papers in the Royal Library in Copenhagen (UF 334, 1).

4 *Strindbergs drömspelteknik – i drama ovh teater* (Lund, 1981), p. 80

5 Cf. Ingrid Hollinger's systematic analysis of Grandinson's lightung in "Urpremiären på *Till Damaskus I*," *Dramaten 175 År: Studier i svansk scenkonst*, ed. Gösta M. Bergman (Stockholm, 1963), pp. 330f.

6 John Nordling in *Idun* 13 (1900), no. 47.

7 August Strindberg, *Brev till Harriet Bosse*, ed. Harriet Bosse (Stockholm, 1932), p. 18.

8 *Thalia* (January 1912), quoted in Hollinger, "Urpremiären på *Till Damaskus*," p. 348.

9 Pär Lagerkvist, *Modern Theatre: Points of View and Attack*, trans. Thomas R. Buckman (Lincoln, Nebraska, 1966), p. 11.

10 Alfred Polgar, *Ja und Nein* (Hamburg, 1956), pp. 45f.

11 Paraphrased in Bark, *Strindbergs drömspelteknik*, p. 95.

12 Siegfried Jacobsohn, *Das Jahr der Bühne* III (Berlin, 1914), p. 182.

13 Bark, *Strindbergs drömspelteknik*, p. 93.

14 Per Lindberg, *Kring ridån* (Stockholm, 1932), p. 142.

15 *Evgeny Vakhtangov*, compiled by Lyubov Vandrovskaya and Galina Kaptereva, trans. Doris Bradbury (Moscow, 1982), pp. 180–81.

16 Lindberg, *Kring ridån*, p. 146.

17 Kristian Elster, *Teater: 1929–1939*, ed. Anton Rønneberg (Oslo, 1941), pp. 155, 159.

18 Quoted in Gunnar Ollén, *Strindbergs dramatik* (Stockholm, 1982), p. 421.

19 Lindberg, *Kring ridån*, p. 136.

20 Martin Lamm, *Strindbergs dramer*, II (Stockholm, 1926), p. 75.

21 *Scenen*, January 1, 1921.

22 "Möten med Strindberg," *Svenska Dagbladet*, January 21, 1949.

23 Agne Beijer, *Teaterrecensioner 1924–1949* (Stockholm, 1954), pp. 245–46.

24 "Regissören är teaterns tusenkonstnär," *Stockholms Tidningen*, December 10, 1922.

25 Beijer, *Teaterrecensioner*, p. 245.

26 Per Erik Wahlund, *Afsidesrepliker: Teaterkritik 1961–1965* (Stockholm, 1966), p. 230.

27 Program dated November 25, 1945. For details on this production, see Lise-Lone Marker and Frederick J. Marker, *Ingmar Bergman: A Life in the Theatre* (Cambridge, 1992), pp. 62–64.

28 Henrik Sjögren in *Arbetet* (Malmö), February 2, 1974.

29 *Scandinavian Review*, 3 (1976), 22–23.

30 Jean-Paul Sartre, "Forgers of Myths," *Theatre Arts Anthology*, eds. Rosamond Gilder, Hermine R. Isaacs and others (New York, 1951), pp. 135–42.

31 See his introduction to August Strindberg, *Selected Plays* (Toronto, 1986), p. 385.

3 A THEATRE OF DREAMS: *A DREAM PLAY*

1 Evert Sprinchorn's translation in his edition of Strindberg, *Selected Plays*, p. 647.
2 Rudolf Björkman in *Scenisk konst*, no. 9 (1907).
3 Strindberg's marked, annotated copy of the Fuchs book is preserved among his papers in the Strindberg Museum in Stockholm.
4 See Falck, *Fem år med Strindberg*, pp. 271–76. These pages, carefully translated by Leif Sjöberg, are found in English in Randolph Goodman, ed. *From Script to Stage: Eight Modern Plays* (New York, 1971), pp. 138–41.
5 Henry Morley, *The Journal of a London Playgoer*, 2nd edn. (London, 1891), p. 57.
6 Jacobsohn, *Das Jahr der Bühne* v (Berlin, 1916), p. 156.
7 *Berliner Zeitung am Mittag*, December 14, 1921.
8 Jacobsohn, *Das Jahr der Bühne* v, p. 157.
9 Egil Törnqvist, "Staging *A Dream Play*," *Strindberg's Dramaturgy*, ed. Göran Stockenström (Minneapolis, 1988), p. 274.
10 Cf. Svend Gade, *Mit Livs Drejescene* (Copnhagen, 1929), pp. 110–15; see also Kela Kvam, *Max Reinhardt og Strindbergs visionære dramatik* (Copenhagen, 1974), pp. 106, 157 n. 10.
11 Sven Lange, *Meninger om Teater* (Copenhagen, 1929), p. 125.
12 Antonin Artaud, *Selected Writings*, ed. Susan Sontag (New York, 1976), pp. 163–64.
13 Quoted in Goodman, *From Script to Stage*, p. 147.
14 Quoted ibid., p. 150.
15 Siegfried Jacobsohn, "Vignettes from Reinhardt's Productions" in *Max Reinhardt and his Theatre*, ed. Oliver M. Sayler (New York, 1924), p. 325.
16 Quoted in Kvam, *Max Reinhardt og Strindbergs visionære dramatik*, p. 107.
17 Klaus van den Berg, "Strindberg's *A Dream Play*: Postmodernist Visions on the Modernist Stage," *Theatre Survey* 40 (November 1999), p. 61.
18 Cf. Kvam, *Max Reinhardt og Strindbergs visionære dramatik*, p. 112. The stage manager's script, marked "Scenen, 1921" (328 pp.), is preserved in the library of Kungliga dramatiska teatern, Stockholm.
19 Kvam, *Max Reinhardt og Strindbergs visionære dramatik*, p. 109. It is not clear from the evidence, however, that this effect was used in practice.
20 Here again the stage manager's script is the better guide to the actual performance.
21 Sprinchorn's introduction to Strindberg, *Selected Plays*, p. 641.
22 Dworsky's working sketches are reproduced in Kvam, *Max Reinhardt og Strindbergs visionære dramatik*, pp. 185–88; there is no hard evidence to indicate how they actually appeared on the stage.
23 Quoted in Kvam, *Max Reinhardt og Strindbergs visionære dramatik*, p. 120.

24 Vagn Børge, *Strindbergs mystiske Teater* (Copenhagen, 1942), p. 283.

25 *Berlingske Tidende* (May 2, 1936); reprinted in Frederik Schyberg, *Ti Aars Teater 1929–1939* (Copenhagen, 1939), p. 141.

26 Bark, *Strindbergs drömspelteknik*, p. 128.

27 Molander's annotated script (p. 67) is found in the library of Kungliga dramatiska teatern, Stockholm.

28 *Perspektiv på teater*, eds. Ulla Gran and Ulla-Britta Lagerroth (Stockholm, 1971), pp. 88–89.

29 Ibid., p. 97.

30 Ibid., p. 98.

31 Letter dated October 29, 1964, printed with other letters in Goodman, *From Script to Stage*, p. 162.

32 Interview with Rut Tellefsen in ibid., p. 163.

33 "Dialog med Ingmar Bergman" in Henrik Sjögren, *Ingmar Bergman på teatern* (Stockholm, 1968), pp. 311–12.

34 "Conversation with Bergman" in John Simon, *Ingmar Bergman Directs* (New York, 1972), pp. 14–15.

35 Quoted in Per Bjurström *Teaterdekoration i Sverige* (Stockholm, 1964), p. 127. Stellan Mörner's stage setting for *Erik XIV* is shown by Bjurström on p. 141.

36 Michael Meyer's translation of the Bergman text, *Strindberg, A Dream Play, Adapted by Ingmar Bergman* (New York, 1971), follows the typed production script exactly. However, the stage directions contained in his translation are not Bergman's and are, in many cases, quite misleading. We have taken details about the staging from the production script, marked *Scenen* (76 pp., Kungliga dramatiska teatern). Other relevant items in Dramaten's library include a ring binder containing some of the director's rehearsal notes.

37 Meyer's translation, p. 54.

38 Ollén, *Strindbergs dramatik*, p. 459.

39 Susan Einhorn, "Directing *A Dream Play*: A Journey through the Waking Dream" in Stockenström, *Strindberg's Dramaturgy*, p. 293.

40 Ibid., p. 296.

41 Lise-Lone Marker and Frederick J. Marker, *Ingmar Bergman: Four Decades in the Theatre* (Cambridge and New York, 1982), p. 221.

42 Ingmar Bergman, *Laterna Magica* (Stockholm, 1987), p. 46. It must be added that the director's depressed account of this particular production's reception does not correspond to the generally favourable tone of its reviews.

43 August Strindberg, *Ett drömspel*, Dramatens spelversion 1986 av Ingmar Bergman (Stockholm, 1986), pp. 114–15.

44 Evert Sprinchorn, *Strindberg as Dramatist* (New Haven, 1982), p. 154.

45 Robert Wilson, "See the Text and Hear the Pictures," *Strindberg, O'Neill and the Modern Theatre: Addresses and Discussions at a Nobel Symposium at the Royal Dramatic Theatre, Stockholm*, eds. Claes Englund and Gunnel Bergström (Stockholm, 1990), pp. 61–62.

4 CHAMBER THEATRE: *THE GHOST SONATA*

1 Robinson, *Strindberg's Letters*, II, p. 892.
2 Quoted in Marker and Marker, *Ingmar Bergman: A Life in the Theatre*, pp. 75–76.
3 Robinson, *Strindberg's Letters*, II, p. 761: letter dated February 2, 1908.
4 Falck, *Fem år med Strindberg*, p. 193.
5 Bark, *Strindbergs drömspelteknik*, p. 87.
6 Reinhardt promptbook, p. 8; quoted in Kvam, *Max Reinhardt og Strindbergs visionære dramatik*, p. 75. This document is an interleaved copy of Schering's 1908 edition of *Gespenstersonate*, marked with copious annotations, diagrams, and sketches, It is found in photocopy form in the Max Reinhardt Forschungs- und Gedänkstätte in Salzburg. The original is held in the Max Reinhardt Archive, State University of New York at Binghamton. However, it is well to recognize that this director's unusually descriptive promptbook notes were, as he himself states in a commentary called *Die Regiebuch*, "written primarily for oneself" and thus do not invariably represent actual performance practice. Cf. Gusti Adler, *Max Reinhardt: Sein Leben* (Salzburg, 1964), pp. 51 f.
7 Reinhardt promptbook, p. 5; quoted in Kvam, *Max Reinhardt og Strindbergs visionære dramatik*, p. 72.
8 Siegfried Jacobsohn, *Max Reinhardt* (Berlin, 1921) p. 80; quoted in J. L. Styan, *Max Reinhardt* (Cambridge and New York, 1982), p. 38.
9 Reinhardt promptbook, p. 8; quoted in Bark, *Strindbergs drömspelteknik*, p. 106.
10 Reinhardt promptbook, p. 34; quoted in Kvam, *Max Reinhardt og Strindbergs visionære dramatik*, p. 78.
11 Jacobsohn, *Das Jahr der Bühne* VI (Berlin, 1917), p. 40.
12 Reinhardt promptbook, p. 31; quoted in Kvam, *Max Reinhardt og Strindbergs visionære dramatik*, p. 82.
13 Promptbook, p. 50; quoted in Kvam, *Max Reinhardt og Strindbergs visionære dramatik*, p. 83.
14 Tschandala, a designation in ancient Indian lore for the lowest Indian caste, became a favourite Nietzschean term for the brutish, ignorant, unworthy side of humanity. As such, it fueled the uncomfortably racist views expressed in Strindberg's novella *Tschandala*, which appeared in 1889. However, Grossmann's linking of this term to the Cook hardly seems relevant to Strindberg's purpose with this character.
15 Cf. Bark, *Strindbergs drömspelteknik*, p. 114.
16 Hakon Wigert-Lundström in *Göteborgs Morgonpost*, May 11, 1917.
17 Kjeld Abell, *Teaterstrejf i Paaskevejr* (Copenhagen, 1962), pp. 33, 37.
18 Agnes Boulton, "An Experimental Theatre," *Theatre Arts Monthly*, March 19, 1924, p. 188.
19 First reprinted *New York Times*, January 6, 1924; also Helen Deutsch and Stella Hanau, *The Provincetown: A Story of the Theatre* (New York, 1931), pp. 191–92.
20 According to costume designer Kyra Markham, quoted in Arthur and Barbara Gelb, *O'Neill* (New York, 1962), p. 537.

21 Eugene Ionesco, *Plays*, trans. Donald Watson (London, 1959), p. ix.

22 Antonin Artaud, *Œuvres complètes*, II (Paris, 1961), p. 113.

23 Anthony Swerling, *Strindberg's Impact in France 1920–1960* (Cambridge: Trinity Lane Press, 1971), p. 180.

24 Quoted in Ollén, *Strindbergs dramatik*, p. 538.

25 *Bonniers litterera magasin* II, no. 9 (Stockholm, 1942), p. 705.

26 Cf. Bark, *Strindbergs drömspelteknik*, p. 146

27 Quoted in Egil Törnqvist, *Bergman och Strindberg: Spöksonaten – drama och iscensättning. Dramaten 1973* (Stockholm, 1973), p. 98. Törnqvist's book contains both a record of rehearsals and a transcription of the production script for this performance.

28 Ollén, *Strindbergs dramatik*, p. 533.

29 Sjögren, *Ingmar Bergman*, p. 146.

30 Quoted in Törnqvist, *Bergman och Strindberg*, p. 226.

31 Törnqvist's transcription in ibid., p. 157. The actual dialogue here is in Evert Sprinchorn's translation.

32 Quoted ibid., p. 107.

33 Typed production script, marked *Scenen*, p. 40 (Kungliga dramatiska teatern). This script and the copy of the production stage manager (Arne Hertler) supply all light, sound, and projection cues.

34 Törnqvist's transcription, p. 151.

35 Hansingvar Hanson suggests these associations in his review in *Stockholms Tidningen* (March 6. 1954).

36 Quoted in Törnqvist, *Bergman och Strindberg*, p. 186.

37 Quoted ibid., p. 192.

38 Quoted ibid., pp. 97–98.

39 Quoted ibid., p. 198.

40 Quoted ibid., p. 102.

41 Gunnar Brandell, "Vad har Bergman gjört av Strindberg?" [What has Bergman done with Strindberg?], *Dagens Nyheter*, February 19, 1974.

42 Quoted in Törnqvist, *Bergman och Strindberg*, p. 192.

43 Quoted ibid., p. 108.

44 Walter R. Fuerst and Samuel J. Hume, *Twentieth-Century Stage Decoration*, I (rpt. New York, 1967), p. 128. Our italics.

45 Convocation address delivered at the University of Toronto, March 22, 1989.

SELECT BIBLIOGRAPHY

Abell, Kjeld. *Teaterstrejf i Paaskevejr*. Copenhagen, 1962.

Adler, Gusti. *Max Reinhardt: Sein Leben*. Salzburg, 1964.

Artaud, Antonin, *Selected Writings*, ed. Susan Sontag. New York, 1976. *Œuvres complètes*, II (Paris, 1961).

Bark, Richard. *Strindbergs drömspelteknik – i drama och teater*. Lund, 1981.

Beijer, Agne. *Teaterrecensioner 1924–1949*. Stockholm, 1954.

Bergman, Gösta M. *Den moderna teaterns genombrott 1890–1925*. Stockholm, 1966. ed. *Dramaten 175 År: Studier i svensk scenkonst*. Stockholm, 1963.

Bergman, Ingmar. *Laterna Magica*. Stockholm, 1987.

Beyer, Nils. *Teaterkvällar 1940–1963*. Stockholm, 1953.

Bjurström, Per. *Teaterdekoration i Sverige*. Stockholm, 1964.

Børge, Vagn. *Strindbergs mystiske Teater*. Copenhagen, 1942.

Brandell, Gunnar. *Strindbergs Infernokris*. Stockholm, 1950.

Brook, Peter. *The Empty Space*. Harmondsworth, Middlesex, 1972.

Cole, Toby, ed. *Playwrights on Playwriting*. New York, 1961.

Cole, Toby and Helen Krich Chinoy, eds. *Directors on Directing*. Indianapolis, 1968.

Deutsch, Helen and Stella Hanau. *The Provincetown: A Story of the Theatre*. New York, 1931.

Elster, Kristian. *Teater: 1929–1939*, ed. Anton Rønneberg. Oslo, 1941.

Evgeny Vakhtangov, compiled by Lyubov Vandrovskaya and Galina Kaptereva, trans. Doris Bradbury. Moscow, 1982.

Falck, August. *Fem år med Strindberg*, 2nd edn. Stockholm, 1935.

Fuerst, Walter R. and Samuel J. Hume. *Twentieth-Century Stage Decoration*, 2 vols. Rpt. New York, 1967.

Gade, Svend. *Mit Livs Drejescene*. Copenhagen, 1941.

Gelb, Arthur and Barbara Gelb. *O'Neill*. New York, 1962.

Gilder, Rosamond, Hermine R. Isaacs, and others, eds. *Theatre Arts Anthology*. New York, 1941.

Goodman, Randolph, ed. *From Script to Stage: Eight Modern Plays*. New York, 1971.

Gran, Ulla and Ulla-Britta Lagerroth, eds. *Perspektiv på teater*. Stockholm, 1971.

Jacobson, Harry. *Strindberg i firsernes København*. Copenhagen, 1948.

Jacobsohn, Siegfried. *Das Jahr der Bühne*, III–VI. Berlin, 1914–17.

Max Reinhardt. Berlin 1921.

Kvam, Kela. *Max Reinhardt og Strindbergs visionære dramatik*. Copenhagen, 1974.

ed. *Strindberg's Post-Inferno Plays*. Copenhagen, 1994.

Lagerkvist, Pär. *Modern Theatre: Points of View and Attack*, trans. Thomas R. Buckman. Lincoln, Nebraska, 1966.

Lamm, Martin. *Strindbergs dramaer*, 2 vols. Stockholm, 1924–26.

Lange, Sven. *Meninger om Teater*. Copenhagen, 1929.

Lindberg, Per. *Kring ridån*. Stockholm, 1932.

Marker, Lise-Lone and Frederick J. Marker. *Ingmar Bergman: Four Decades in the Theatre*. Cambridge and New York, 1982.

Ingmar Bergman: A Life in the Theatre. Cambridge and New York, 1992.

Meyer, Michael. *Strindberg: A Biography*. London, 1985.

ed. and trans. *Strindberg, A Dream Play, Adapted by Ingmar Bergman*. New York, 1971.

Molander, Olof. *Detta är jag . . .* Stockholm, 1961.

Ollén, Gunnar. *Strindbergs dramatik*. Stockholm, 1982.

Polgar, Alfred. *Ja und Nein*. Hamburg, 1956.

Robinson, Michael, ed. *Strindberg's Letters*. 2 vols. Chicago and London, 1992.

Studies in Strindberg. Norwich, 1998.

Sayler, Oliver M., ed. *Max Reinhardt and his Theatre*. New York, 1924.

Schyberg, Frederik. *Ti Aars Teater 1929–1939*. Copenhagen, 1939.

Shakespearean Continuities: Essays in Honour of E.A.J. Honigmann, eds. John Batchelor, Tom Caine, and Claire Lamont. London and New York, 1997.

Simon, John. *Ingmar Bergman Directs*. New York, 1971.

Sjögren, Henrik. *Ingmar Bergman på teatern*. Stockholm, 1968.

Smedmark, Carl Reinhold, ed. *August Strindbergs dramaer*. 4 vols. Stockholm, 1962–70.

Sprinchorn, Evert. *Strindberg as Dramatist*. New Haven, 1982.

Stockenström, Göran, ed. *Strindberg's Dramaturgy*. Minneapolis, 1988.

Strindberg, August. *Brev*, eds. Torsten Eklund and Björn Meidal. 19 vols. Stockholm, 1948–94.

Brev til Harriet Bosse, ed. Harriet Bosse. Stockholm, 1932.

Miss Julie and Other Plays, ed. and trans. Michael Robinson. Oxford and New York, 1998.

Open Letters to the Intimate Theatre, trans. Walter Johnson. Seattle, 1967.

Samlade skrifter, ed. John Landquist. 55 vols. Stockholm, 1912–21. [Superseded by *Nationalupplagen av August Strindbergs samlade verk*, 72 vols. Stockholm, 1981 –. 57 volumes of the total edition are now in print or in press.]

Selected Plays, ed. and trans. Evert Sprinchorn. Toronto, 1986.

The Son of a Servant, trans. Evert Sprinchorn. Garden City, NY, 1966.

Strindberg, O'Neill and the Modern Theatre: Addresses and Discussions at a Nobel Symposium at the Royal Dramatic Theatre, Stockholm, eds. Claes Englund and Gunnel Bergström. Stockholm, 1990.

Styan, J. L. *Max Reinhardt*. Cambridge and New York, 1982.

Törnqvist, Egil. *Bergman och Strindberg: Spöksonaten – drama och iscensättning*. Stockholm, 1973.

Törnqvist, Egil and Barry Jacobs. *Strindberg's Miss Julie: A Play and Its Transcriptions*. Norwich, 1988.

Waal, Carla Rae. *Harriet Bosse, Strindberg's Wife and Interpreter*. Carbondale, 1990.

Wahlund, Per-Erik. *Afsidesrepliker: Teaterkritik 1961–1865*. Stockholm, 1966. *Scenväxling: Teaterkritik 1954–1960*.

INDEX